A WORLD OF DIFFERENCE

Wales & Western England
Edited by Genya Beeby

 Young**Writers**

First published in Great Britain in 2008 by:
Young Writers
Remus House
Coltsfoot Drive
Woodston
Peterborough
PE2 9JX
Telephone: 01733 890066
Website: www.youngwriters.co.uk

SB ISBN 978-1 84431 775 2

Foreword

Young Writers' Big Green Poetry Machine is a showcase for our nation's most brilliant young poets to share their thoughts, hopes and fears for the planet they call home.

Young Writers was established in 1990 to nurture creativity in our children and young adults, to give them an interest in poetry and an outlet to express themselves. Seeing their work in print will encourage them to keep writing as they grow, and become our poets of tomorrow.

Selecting the poems has been challenging and immensely rewarding. The effort and imagination invested by these young writers makes their poems a pleasure to enjoy reading time and time again.

Contents

Blessed Edward Jones Catholic High School, Rhyl

Moreton Hall, Oswestry
Honor Amy Turpin (12)   50
Lauren Howe (13)   51

Nantyglo Comprehensive School, Nantyglo
Darian Duggan (12)   51
Rebecca Koash (13)   52
Joshua Griffiths (11)   52
Kirsty Allison (13)   53
Lewis Hodges (12)   53
Hope Ayeisha Victoria Meek (12) 54
Phoebe Bridge (12)   54
Tori Williams (12)   55
Rhys Evans (12)   55
Morgan Jenkins (13)   56
Connor Griffiths (13)   57

Pengwern Residential College, Rhyl
Kyle Winterbottom (20)   57
Teresa Walley & Diane Lee (17) 58

Round Oak School, Warwick
Lewis Berry (15)   58

Tenbury High School, Tenbury Wells
Jack Moran (11)   58
Zoe Leadbetter (12)   59
Chloe Gittins (12)   59
Alice Withers (12)   59
Martin Bailey (12)   60
Anthony Cook (11)   60
Hannah Hopkinson (13)   60
Tommy Village (11)   61
Alice Waite (13)   61
Lucas Tisdale (13)   61
Georgie Bufton (11)   62
Joe Webb (12)   62
Amy Byers (12)   63
Jasmine Bibby (12)   63
Leanne Potter (12)   63

Georgie Clark (12) 64
Emma Nicholls (12) 64
James Lloyd (14) 65
Richard Strawford (12) 65
Jordan Powell (12) 66
David Parsons (12) 66
Natalie Nicholls-Lamb (15) 67
Christie James (12) 67
Bethan Dennis (12) 68
Kate Yarnold (12) 68
Carla Dallow (13) 68
Declan Morbey (11) 69
Katherine Whistance (12) 69
Scott Dallow (12) 70
Ben Jordan (12) 70
Ellie Mapp (12) 70
Tara Nicholls (12) 71
Amy Miles (12) 71
Jonquil Ives (13) 71
Bethany Hayward (12) 72
Clare Kerby (13) 72
Jess Sanders (12) 73
Francesca Jones (13) 73
Dan Pitt (11) 74
Lindsay Perkins (11) 74
Jack Houchin (13) 74
Anna Günther (12) 75
Alice Pollard (13) 75
Callum Redding (12) 76
Becky Tomkins Bevan (12) 77
Emily Holland (12) 78

The Corbet School Technology College, Baschurch
Isobel Goodman (12) 79

The Cotswold School, Bourton-on-the-Water
Amy Hayes (14) 80
Emilia McIntyre (13) 81
Charlotte Green (14) 81
Ruby Fenton (14) 82
Ben Glass (15) 82

Laura Martin (14)	83
Sophie Witt (13)	83
Tess Simpson (14)	84
Iain York (15)	85
Sophie Mustoe (14)	86
Hannah Davis (14)	87
Ellie James (15)	88
Ryan Evans (15)	88
Rebecca Howard (14)	89
Jamie Goddard (13)	89
Jack Howarth (15)	90
Ben Brown (13)	91
Becky Emes (14)	92

Whitecross High School, Hereford

Annie Riach (12)	92
Lauren Marissa Taylor (11)	93
Sarah Mann (12)	93
Madeleine Roffey (11)	94
Jack Stenhouse (12)	94
Laura Watson (12)	95
Emilia Booth (12)	95
Vicki Jones (12)	96
Mia Leak (12)	96
Lewis Pearce (12)	97
William Penson (12)	97
Jordan Briscoe (12)	98
Adam Williams (12)	99
Jess Preece (12)	100
Felix Rogers (12)	100
Caitlin Chilman (12)	101
Alex Martin (12)	101
Hallum Prendergast (12)	102
Aaron Gilligan (11)	102
Lewis Rogers (12)	103
Jack Parkes (12)	103
Poppy Williams (12)	104
Jack Allen (12)	104
Naomi Kemp (12)	105
Kori Lee (12)	105
Carys Kenyon (12)	106

Oliver Deakin (12)   106
Jordan Lambourn (11)   107
Holly Weaver (11)   107
Abbie Blake (12)   108
Tyler Westlake (12)   109
Charley-Jennifer Mead (12)   109
Lucien Barsacq (12)   110
Adam Andrews (12)   110
Emma Alty (12)   110
Joshua Rees (12)   111

Wigmore High School, Leominster

Harriet Hodnett (11)   111
Steve Juson (12)   111
Josh Barber (12)   112
Elliot Sparrow (12)   112
Jack Clayton (11)   113
Heulwen Gilbert (12)   113
Danielle Johnston (12)   114
Laura Johnson (12)   114
Jordan Bufton (12)   114
Julia Byatt (12)   115
Molly Bashford (12)   115
Zoe Priday (11)   116
Eilish Gilbert (12)   116
James Phillips (12)   117
Matthew Beaumont-Pike (11)   117
Rhian Stevens (12)   118
Amy Cave-Browne-Cave (12)   119
Jay Thomas Warner (12)   120

The Poems

The Shrinking World

As icebergs disappear.
As temperatures rise,
We all stand in fear
As the world slowly dies!

Recycle and reuse,
We hear it everyday,
But we never seem to lose
The urge to throw away.

Drop it on the floor,
The effort is a sin,
Just to take the extra steps
To put it in the bin.

Is it a cloud all across the sky?
Or could it be fog?
Look at the traffic and think why,
That dirty cloud is smog.

Ethan Young (13)
Afon Taf High School, Merthyr Tydfil

The World At War

Guns, bombs and fighter planes,
All will lose and none will gain,
Again we'll have to face the blackout,
Wondering if we'll ever get out.

Another tyrant will reign again,
We may all be dead by 2010,
All men will go to fight,
We won't be able to sleep at night.

What if they drop a nuclear missile?
No shelter for over a mile,
This is why war is not a good thing,
In harmony the world should sing.

Carwyn Chamberlain (13)
Afon Taf High School, Merthyr Tydfil

Rainforest

The Amazon is dying and loggers are to blame,
They may as well stop and hang their heads in shame.

For every tree that dies, one person chokes,
It doesn't matter if you're a Sheila or a bloke.

You're killing people with paper and mahogany,
Those tribal people are living in agony.

Animals will die, birds and monkeys,
So to save them all ditch the car keys.

These things make me angry, helpless and sad,
Haven't these people learned good from bad?

For the monkeys in the trees, birds on the canopy,
I speak for Earth, 'Please help me!'

Reduce, reuse, recycle, can all be done,
To save the rainforest for everyone.

Daniel Morgan (12)
Afon Taf High School, Merthyr Tydfil

Untitled

I am getting really annoyed
That our world is being destroyed.
Homeless people on the street,
Walking around with bare feet.
Gangs and crime surround our city,
Don't they feel any pity?

Litter makes our streets a mess,
We need to throw away less.
Reuse, reduce, recycle,
We all need to learn how to cycle!

Think about the poor,
We have so much more,
But we are wasting it.

Bronwen James & Hannah Minney (14)
Afon Taf High School, Merthyr Tydfil

Our World

Rainforests with their tall trees
get demolished by the seas.
For pollution
we need a solution.

Animals of extinction,
cost no creation.
We need to stop war
because it's not a chore.

Trying to help the homeless
has been very hopeless.
The climate is changing,
so we need some rearranging.

Start recycling
and help by cycling.
People who litter
are very bitter.

Yasmin Ames (14)
Afon Taf High School, Merthyr Tydfil

Stop The Racism

We live in one world
which is beautiful and great,
why we have to fight
is what I really hate.

We are all special
in our own unique way,
it doesn't matter what colour,
size, religion, I say.

We should all live together,
no matter who we are
and stop the wars forever
and love the world we share.

Nia Randall (12)
Afon Taf High School, Merthyr Tydfil

Save The Animals

What can you do to help the animals?
Have you ever thought
Of how those poor bears suffer
Because of what we've caused?
Or how tigers are hunted
For no other reason than greed?
Or how the panda can't survive
Because mankind must succeed?
These wild and wonderful creatures
Deserve a happy life too,
Unlike those heavy-hearted ones
Man stuffs inside a zoo.
I can't imagine a world
Without gorillas or eagles or whales.
Protect them, please, for us today,
Let's hope that we don't fail.

Jennifer Kate Gill (12)
Afon Taf High School, Merthyr Tydfil

Fair Day's Wage

Money's scarce
No food to eat
Hunger hard to beat

Out early in the morning
In late at night
Working hard for next to nothing

Can't support my family
Can't feed my children
Can only just keep my house

All I want is a fair day's wage
For a day's work
To get my family out of this slum.

Rachel Tudor (13)
Afon Taf High School, Merthyr Tydfil

If Rainforests Could Talk . . .

If rainforests could talk,
There would be constant talk of the suffering animals
Who struggle to find homes in the forest
Known to all as paper/wood source except for these:
    Hunting
        Protecting
            Surviving.

If rainforests could talk,
There would be endless moaning over the
Uncontrollable hot, humid weather
As it rains heavily onto the massive leaves of the dense forest:
    Pouring
        Flooding
            Drowning.

If rainforests could talk,
There would be continuous crying,
Drowned out by shadows of the night sky
Setting over a lonesome forest,
With death upon itself,
Because of pollution, fumes in the atmosphere,
Demolition, harmful substances, disease
And your carbon footprint:
    Global warming
        End of living
            Helpless.

Abbie Bolitho (13)
Afon Taf High School, Merthyr Tydfil

Nowhere To Go

Young ones want to go out and go some place,
Now I can go out, but there's nowhere to go.

No roof over my head, no food to eat,
It's a hard living life on the street.

There's only one of me, yet there's thousands more,
Who wait on the streets, outside a store.

Why won't someone let me in?
I mean, that's not exactly committing a sin.

Elizabeth Barnes (13)
Afon Taf High School, Merthyr Tydfil

The Big Green Machine

There was a big green machine
that was barely ever mean
when you put things in
it would jiggle and spin.
But then along came the bin,
the big green machine
started to turn mean.
But the bin changed weather
which changed the world forever.
The green machine turned very mad
so the children were very sad
because their world had turned so bad.
'We need to recycle,' shouted the green machine.
The children agreed with a big white gleam,
put the paper in there
and the cardboard in the box
because recycling is here!

Ffion Rowlands (14)
Alun School, Mold

Racism

Do you want to be like everyone else?
Do you get bullied because of who you are?
All you need to do is be yourself.
Get out of the house, don't hide behind the door.

Wherever your place of worship,
Or the colour of your skin,
It's what is on the inside
Which is good, not sin.

If you're made to feel like an outcast,
You shouldn't listen to the kids at school.
You are a respectable person,
They are just cruel.

Be proud of your colour and what you believe,
Show your courage, do not leave.
You're individual, but not too unique,
Respect will not be difficult to seek.
Just believe!

Kristina Waxler (13)
Alun School, Mold

Less Time To Live

Wasting energy adds to pollution,
Pollution adds to climate change,
Climate change kills animals and rainforests.
Recycling lessens pollution,
Less pollution slows climate change,
Less climate change saves plants and animals from extinction.

The less we do to help the planet the less time we have to live.
The less we do to solve poverty the more children die.
The less we care for the environment the less animals exist.

Steven Costidell (14)
Alun School, Mold

Our Planet

We pollute the Earth with no thought or care,
We damage the ozone, this cannot be fair.
We drive our cars which puff out smoke,
That pollutes the air and makes us choke.

On our Earth we have different races,
From Europeans to Asians and other nations.
We fight our wars through men with toys,
Which brings no justice nor any joy.
The innocent are yet to fall,
But the time will come
If we carry on with these wars.

We should recycle to help the Earth,
To keep it breathing, this it deserves.
So let's do our bit and give it a go,
Start recycling and help Mother Nature's soul.

Kayleigh Williams (13)
Alun School, Mold

The Pain Of It

Every day, life of the people in poverty
They can only explain themselves.

The pain and the strain of having no money,
A good night's rest without any worries.

Wanting the nightmare to end
But cannot wake up.

Cold night sweats,
Faint sound of a heartbeat,
Dark, heavy eyes,
And hard, aching feet.
No options to take,
No plans to make,
Just a taster of the pain in poverty!

Shannon Bonar (13)
Alun School, Mold

The World's Fate

Our world is full of people,
Some very smart and clever,
But you don't have to be smart
To know the world won't last forever.

People drink a can of coke on the bicycle,
But when they finish it goes on the ground,
When they should recycle.

People are being sent to war,
But now it's becoming a giant bore.

What's the point of all this fighting?
The cities that the terrorists are igniting?

To think what's going to happen next I hate,
What is to become of our world's fate.

Ben Breach-Cannon (13)
Alun School, Mold

Horribly Homeless

I'm hungry,
I'm thirsty,
I'm lonely,
I'm cold,
I may not be very old and I'm sure not bold,
But I know that not everyone lives like me.
Spending my nights under a tree,
Exposed to the rain and the snow and the thunder.
I lie late at night, I think and I wonder
What it would be like to have food in the freezer,
Or to be able to just use my own Visa.
I'm poor,
I'm dirty,
I'm sick
I'm homeless.

Molly Austen (13)
Alun School, Mold

The Green Machine

Brightly coloured recycling bins danced around until May,
They were used by everyone, until one day,
The shiny black bag sat there with a grinning face.
Within seconds people said he was ace.
The unwanted recycling bin went to a quiet place.

Tall trees stood proudly for everybody to see,
Amongst them lived the chimpanzee.
The wicked machine sat there and stared,
Within seconds the machine said, 'Full speed ahead!'
All the trees and animals were dead.

The sparkling, shimmering street smiled,
A can was dropped by a child,
Rubbish here and there, the people had gone wild.
People stopped caring about the world, they became bitter,
Then the streets became full of litter.

The super, green machine came out to save the day,
He said, 'Get out of my way!'
The black bag, wicked machine and litter wouldn't move,
The super, green machine got down to business; to remove.
A sparkling new world emerged and continued to improve.

Anokhi Patel (13)
Alun School, Mold

Our Life

Some people are racist towards other people
But it doesn't matter what colour you are
You could be black or white, it doesn't matter
You could have light or dark hair, people don't care
As long as you don't care, that'll be fair.

People drop litter on the streets
But then they realise when we meet
Litter is dangerous to animals and humans
Animals can die and humans can suffer
So don't drop litter, bin the litter!

Lauren Morris (13)
Alun School, Mold

War

For centuries blood has been shed by killers,
But they're not the only blood-spillers.
Innocent lives have been lost,
Which comes at an enormous cost.

The terrifying experience of war
Has left mourners' hearts feeling sore.
Even brothers fight brothers and friends,
They keep killing
Until wars end.

Countries in conflict are like an evil board game,
But no joy comes from them, just shame.
We could stop this conflict once and for all
And then our great nation can stand tall.

Next time you see a war memorial
Think carefully about the loss of lives in war,
Maybe you can stop the bloodshed
From becoming more.

Helena Bronwen Lewis (14)
Alun School, Mold

Our World Is Dying

The rainforests are coming down at a scary rate.
But that's just one of the things in this crazy world
That I have come to hate.

People not recycling are filling up the landfill sites.
Then there's racism and religion, causing so many fights.
Pollution, we are making our Earth choke.
Greenhouse gases covering it, like a giant cloak.

This is all happening because no one's really trying.
We'd better get a move on though
Because our world is dying!

Matthew Bircham (13)
Alun School, Mold

Stop The Bullying

There is no problem with what colour you are,
Black or white, we're both the same.
Ginger or blond, it's only a hair colour.

Please recycle, it will help our future,
Recycle bags,
Bin rubbish,
Recycle glass,
Don't smash it.

Grace Lawson (13)
Alun School, Mold

Pollution

P ollution affects everyone
O h, my gosh!
L itter is one of the main causes of pollution
L ots of people choose to ignore pollution
U niverse is under threat
T ogether we can make a difference
I gloos are melting
O zone layer is broken, heating up our world
N ow we have started it, how can we stop it?

Ollie Marshall (14)
Alun School, Mold

Litter

L ittering is bad
I t wrecks the landscape
T he animals eat it
T he animals die from it
E nough of this horrible pollution
R unning out of time for animals.

Gareth Jones (12)
Alun School, Mold

What Can You See?

Some people they travel by boat,
Some people they travel by car,
Just look around you and can't you see,
Polluters, that's what we are.

There is a world to see,
When you're home, watching TV,
Or on your PS3,
Waiting for your mum to finish your tea.

Why can't we travel on foot
And see the beautiful sights?
But no, we travel by car,
All cramped up tight.

Now look in the mirror
And what do you see?
Are you in a wonderful place
Or in this world I can see?

Sophie Greatbatch (13)
Alun School, Mold

Recycling

R ecycling is a burden we all share
E ngland is really cursed with
C ans left, crisp packets everywhere
Y oghurt lids floating and stink bombs bursting
C ommittees trying to stop it
L avatories still smell rank
I find the smell's still there
N oticed the rubbish is slowly disappearing
G oing so well, don't stop now.
    Recycle!

Lewis Riley (12)
Avon Valley School, Rugby

Waiting

The bitter litter that lies on the ground,
Waiting, waiting to be found.

The innocent, beautiful, colourful birds
Waddle along and choke and choke,
Waiting, waiting to be heard.

The homeless man that wishes to be fed,
If he doesn't eat he'll soon be dead,
Waiting, waiting, 'Someone help,' he said.

The factories and planes so high in the sky,
Stop the pollution or else the world will die,
Waiting, waiting for a reply . . .

No answer, no answer . . .
Say bye-bye.

Chloe Evans-Essam (11)
Avon Valley School, Rugby

Scared Of Change

Why did the world have to change?
Why do we have war and climate change?
Why do people live on the streets?
Why do people in Africa have no food to eat?
Why are animals dying out?
Why isn't it safe to go out and about?
Why are children bullied at school?
Why is there so much trouble about?
Now all I want to do is shout,
'Why are you people ruining our world?
Please stop, I'm only a little girl!
I have all my life ahead,
But how can I see the world when I'm dead?'

Holly Louise White (12)
Avon Valley School, Rugby

War

War is a terrible thing,
The sounds of guns shooting,
All of the soldiers dying
And all of their families crying.

Gunshots in the winter night's air,
The dazzling sparkles of the flares,
But all you may know about war,
Is the soldiers who fall to the floor.

The families are asking why,
Why did their children have to die?
Then they go back to their weeping,
While the blackbirds are cheeping.

War is a terrible thing,
The sounds of guns shooting,
All of the soldiers dying
And all of their families crying.

Kyle Cooper (12)
Avon Valley School, Rugby

Recycling

Shout about all down the streets,
Start recycling paper sheets.
Then recycle tins and cans,
Then reuse pots and pans.

Reduce the amounts you chuck in your bins,
Recycle in your red box and win.
The Earth is home to all of us,
So save the Earth for the rest of us.

Shout about all down the streets,
Start recycling paper sheets.
Pollution grows every day,
So get out of your car and ride your bike,
That is what the Earth would like.

Daniel Prior (12)
Avon Valley School, Rugby

Climate Change

Climate change is really bad,
It makes me very sad.
The government are building all over the countryside,
It is driving me mad.

When all this rubbish is over, I will be very glad,
But this will not happen unless you put out that fag.
All that smoke going high, right up to the big, blue sky,
It's melting away at the ice and that is not very nice.

Andrew Howes (12)
Avon Valley School, Rugby

Racism

Racism is a crime that should not be done.
Racism is something that is not much fun.
Racism is sad and racism is cruel.
Racism is something that happens in your school.
Racism is something that will not go away.
Racism is something that happens every day.
If you're a victim and want something done,
Do your part, before racism's won!

Bethany Richmond (12)
Avon Valley School, Rugby

Extinction

Tigers, pandas, rhinos too,
Polar bears, penguins, not the kangaroo.
Elephants, dolphins, lions, gorillas,
Leather-back turtles, not the armadillos.
All of these animals are vulnerable from
Poaching and hunting.
You must stop it - *now!*

Hollie Burrell (12)
Avon Valley School, Rugby

Pollution

In a flash my story goes,
About some smoke that nobody knows.
It rises, rises, right up into the air,
When it did it gave me a scare.

So what are we going to do?
Although the government already knew,
Why not go *eco!* Why not go *green!*
So then the world will not go mean.

Matthew Moseley (14)
Avon Valley School, Rugby

Animals

A lways being hunted down
N ever being left to roam around
I 've never seen it like this before
M ove on from the hunting ages
A ll being killed for fun or food
L et them live the life we do
S o stop now and let them live too.

Zachariah George
Avon Valley School, Rugby

Go Green

G oing past cars
O ver the hill

G oing to pollute the world
R eady to breathe carbon
E xcuses for killing
E nvironment dying
N ow think and go green!

Jenny White (13)
Avon Valley School, Rugby

Going Green

One day has passed
It is going so fast
People dying
Planes are flying
No clue what's coming next
So we just carry on
One day we will have nothing
It's only just begun

The weather is changing
So are we
People becoming ill
And leaving a will

One day we will be a speck
And the Earth will be a wreck
Global warming is coming
Save yourself now!
Go green!

Chloe Herbert
Avon Valley School, Rugby

Recycle

Start to recycle tins and cans,
Paper, card, pots and pans.
Trees are starting to run out,
Turn to green and shout about.

Our planet's dying,
Its long-lived life is flying,
Its death is drawing near,
The future is unclear.

It looks the time to start anew,
A brand new start for me and you.
Let's all run the race for life,
Win it now and end our strife.

James Fiddament-Harris (12)
Avon Valley School, Rugby

Homeless

I'm lonely and frightened
But scared and enlightened
There's children out there
But does anyone know where?
They're all in rags
Or even old bags
They find food when they can
Or ask a woman or man
There's plenty of litter
And it's cold and bitter
Can we find a way
To stop this in May?
There's awful smells
Which comes from wells
The drains are full
Of something like wool
Will we find a way
To stop this in May?
Please, please say
There is a way.

Leah Anderson-Howe (12)
Avon Valley School, Rugby

Black As Smoke

P ollution grows every day
O ily roads break my way
L ots of lorries creating smoke
L ungs that are as black as coke
U nderneath the heavy rails
T rains that litter steel nails
I n the clouds, in the sky
O ld birds flying high
N o one knows how to fix it
    everybody needs to help.

Tobias Woodley (12)
Avon Valley School, Rugby

Global Warming

Global warming,
Rain is pouring,
The sun is boiling
And trouble is toiling.

500 degrees,
burning the trees,
ice-caps are melting,
like an ice cream helping.

People burning,
The sun is turning,
Night is easing
And it's flipping freezing.

The heat is boiling our blood,
It's too hot for us all,
But there is one solution,
We gotta stop pollution.

Pearse Macleod
Avon Valley School, Rugby

Environment

E co-houses are the best
N ever drop litter on the floor
V ans we stop and we walk
I gloos are melting because of us
R ecycle your cans and paper
O ur world is in our hands
N ever give up
M e and you can do it
E nvironment . . . don't forget
N ever shall we back down
T rash I don't like.

Karl Clusker (12)
Avon Valley School, Rugby

Our World

Climate change makes us regret
All the things we can't forget.

Racism is out there,
We have to be fair.

Everyone should have a house,
Everyone, every mouse.

Pollution fills our air,
We should take much more care.

Rainforests falling,
Animals calling,

Litter is all around,
Everywhere, every ground.

This is our world that we live in,
Let's try and change!

Charlotte Wilson (12)
Avon Valley School, Rugby

Go Green

G o green.
R ecycle; cans, plastic, paper.
E co-friendly
E nvironmentally friendly.
N ever waste things.

W orld needs saving.
O zone layer disintegrating.
R euse things.
L ike the world.
D o your duty!

Lawrence Colmer (14)
Avon Valley School, Rugby

Litter

Litter on the ground.
Litter in the sky.
Litter far away.
Litter nearby.

Litter in the sea.
Litter in the air.
Litter on the floor.
Litter everywhere!

All of those dying animals,
Choking on our garbage,
So we can all do our bit
To help prevent it!

Recycle all of your garbage,
Sweetie wrappers and empty jam jars.
Plastic bags and glass milk bottles,
Paper, plastic and sweetie jars.

So if you are near a recycling bin,
Whether you are walking or cycling,
If you have any litter nearby,
Just don't bin it, do the recycling.

Harry Phillips (11)
Avon Valley School, Rugby

Turning Green

T urn off unneeded lights
U se renewable energy
R ecycle your rubbish
N ever waste water.

G et insulation in your homes
R educe, reuse, recycle
E nvironmentally friendly
E veryone has their part to play to have a clean planet
N ow clean the planet, it's your child's future at stake.

Christopher Harris
Avon Valley School, Rugby

Global Warming's Effects

2020, there's a giant flood,
Crashing water mixed in with mud.
The entire world is in trouble,
We'd better sort out this mess, on the double.

All this talk makes me mad,
I never thought things would be so bad.
The world shouldn't end this way,
Let's stop this now, but I have more to say.

There's rubbish overflowing
And not much chance of it going.
Up to our necks with filthy, stinking litter.
This taste that lingers is not sweet, it's bitter.

The answer is easy,
Clean up your mess.
Try to recycle as well,
Help lose the distress.

Crescent Franklin (12)
Avon Valley School, Rugby

Pollution

Pollution these days, no one seems to care.
Just take the time to look around you, can you see it anywhere?
The local cement works, even pet food factories,
Cars, buses, big company lorries,
Things like this need to slow down.
I've had enough of seeing them when I look around.
Animals are dying, due to loss of their homes,
The ozone layer is disappearing from Earth.
Ice caps are melting, no one knows what to do.
Everyone must do their part,
That's including you!

Kyle Gibson
Avon Valley School, Rugby

Poverty

There are people all around us,
People everywhere,
People with no money,
With no one for them to care.

They can't afford houses,
So they live in the street,
In damp, cramped spaces,
With really sore feet.

People just walk past them,
As though they are not there,
Just minding their own business,
They couldn't really care.

So now you know the meaning,
The meaning of that word,
The one where there is no laughter
And no one will be heard.

Tegan Skues
Avon Valley School, Rugby

Global Warming

G oing green
L orries polluting
O zone layer disappearing
B oats leaking oil
A nimals in danger from loss of trees
L ots of cars on the road.

W hat's going to happen next?
A re we killing the world?
R ecycle your rubbish
M ethane from cows
I don't want global warming in my life
N o more global warming
G lobal warming's got to stop.

Charlotte Smith
Avon Valley School, Rugby

Litter

When I walk down the street
It all crowds around my feet.
Rubbish is not here and there,
It's absolutely everywhere.

It shoots along the floor,
A half-eaten apple core.
Along it rolls and rolls
And gets squished under soles.

A crisp packet rustles by
And floats up into the sky.
Someone must have thrown it down,
Now it'll go from town to town.

The world is changing fast,
It wasn't like this in the past.
The government need to do something,
Litter, pollution, everything.

Emma Whiteside
Avon Valley School, Rugby

Go Green

Go green and recycle,
Don't drive just cycle.
This all started because of pollution,
Now it's causing all destruction.

Eat the healthy,
Not the bad.
It makes you feel better
And not so sad.

Save the world,
Make a difference.
Go green
And be different!

Summer Stewardson (14)
Avon Valley School, Rugby

Anti-Litter

One day I saw a litterbug,
Just walking down the street.
He dropped his litter on the floor,
It landed by my feet.

I stopped to have a talk with him,
He turned and walked away.
So I said, 'Hey, you stupid man,
You'll kill us all one day.'

He turned around and said to me,
'What is wrong with you?'
I turned around and said to him,
'It's the wrapper you just threw.'

So then he picked it up again
And threw it at my head.
'If you do that once again,
I'll do something that you'll dread.'

Next I dragged him down the street
And put him into jail.
'Let me out, I did nothing wrong.'
The man began to wail.

So now the man has done his time,
So now the man is free.
Put your litter in a bin,
Come on, don't waste a tree!

Kyle Wright (13)
Avon Valley School, Rugby

My Changing The World Poem

Children, adults everywhere,
I'll tell you why we all should care,
Doing stuff to help each other,
Could really make you feel much better.

You see a boy upon the floor,
Staring at an apple core,
People stare as they walk past,
Why does the world have to change so fast?

People make remarks as they see him,
They don't care that he looks so thin.
People show that they don't care,
By spitting food into his hair.

He looks so ill, so crooked and weak,
Opening his eyes to have a peek,
He sees someone above him with a big black hood,
Will he get away; he would if he could.

He lies there all alone, on the damp of the street,
Praying to God for something good to eat.
His health isn't brilliant, neither is his arm,
He needs some care and some peace and calm.

The world is changing, oh so fast,
It's nothing like it was in the past.
I wish things were better and we were all equal
And that we could get on with all people.

Leah-Jade Ward
Avon Valley School, Rugby

Desperation

See the man upon the street,
Litter blows around his feet
Sadly snorting his cocaine,
He thinks that it will cure the pain.

See the girl with curly hair,
Skirt and boots pulled up there.
She sells herself to pay the rent,
It's not her fault, it's how things went.

See the boy who cries each night,
Bottles up his pain and fright.
Scared that when his dad comes home,
He'll beat him and bruise him to the bone.

See the teen inside the shop,
Stuffing fags inside her top.
She doesn't care about her cough,
She hopes the alarms will not go off.

So count yourself lucky you don't live this way,
You always wake up to a brighter day.
You can escape this life with a simple vacation,
But for some, life is nothing but desperation.

Sara Danielle Cecilia Krause
Avon Valley School, Rugby

Green Grass

Green, green, green grass
You won't be so green when the years pass,
Because of global warming,
Say bye-bye to the morning.
You were green but turned brown,
Because the snow put you down,
You love it when the sun's out,
So please give me a shout,
Green, green, green grass.

Katie Randle (14)
Avon Valley School, Rugby

The Next Generation

I think we should clean up the nation,
Nice and tidy for our next generation.
Lots of pollution in traffic jams;
Attacking babies in their prams.

Filling their lungs with toxic gasses,
Lots of landfills with rubbish in masses.
Let's have a ban on smoking cigars and fags
And stop using plastic shopping bags!

The sea level rises, fast and high,
Energy saving light bulbs we must buy.
Polar bears and penguins both in danger,
This matter is definitely *major!*
So put rubbish in the bin,
Because destroying the world is a sin!

Tom Swindell
Avon Valley School, Rugby

A Green Earth

If you want the world to last forever
You'd best get your act together.
Walk don't use the car
If you want to go to the bar.
Turn off your lights during the day,
Then you can go out to play.
Help save the Earth
By not watching the Smurfs.
Don't waste your electricity
Or you'll be busy.
So be eco-friendly,
So the Earth can be healthy.

Gianni Brigginshaw
Avon Valley School, Rugby

Recycle

Put the plastic in the bin
And you'll do a good thing.
Things should get better
If we work together.

You'll see the cycle
For the will to recycle,
That little man -
Holdin' a can.

Are there people now
With the know-how
To keep the world from
Blowing up, like a big bomb?

So pick up that can
And help the recycle man.
So simply -
Pick up a can!

Sean McCabe
Avon Valley School, Rugby

Rainforests

In Borneo and Mexico
The Amazon and Africa,
Forests lay there forever,
Only to be destroyed.

If you want to keep them living,
Don't knock them down,
Let the rainforests live forever
And do the world proud.

Meg Kardasz (12)
Avon Valley School, Rugby

Eco-Friendly

E nough is enough
C an't we stop
O ffences to the Earth.

F rom England to China
R evise your electricity usage
I will do the same
E lectricity is going quickly
N o one needs TV
D efinitely not the PC
L ike me, help the Earth to be healthy
Y ou can make a difference.

Jack Prosser
Avon Valley School, Rugby

How Can You . . .

How can you watch me die of hunger
Then continue to throw out food?
While I lie here *full* of starvation,
With my mouth as dry as a desert.

How can you long for so much more
When already you have enough?
But with me it is a different story,
All my clothes are tattered and torn
And the fields you walk on I use as my bed.

How can you get on with your life
Muffling out my voice?
As I am shouting as loud as I can,
Too bad your ignorance is stopping you from listening.

Continue as you are now,
As I am shouting no more.
I'm in a happier place with my parents now,
My friends are here too;
You know, in that place above.

Lebogang Makati (13)
Blessed Edward Jones Catholic High School, Rhyl

The End

What has the world come to?
I wish I knew!
Everywhere is silent and dead,
why so quiet? I ask myself,
where is everybody?
I walk past the stone-cold water and tremble with fear,
the silky sea of Black Burrow Bay.
It is both as soft as a blanket
but as hard as rock!
Huh! This must be it.
The core of Black Burrow Bay is finally dying.
The sound waves are now travelling through the vacuum of space
and through my own body!
Until . . . *swoosh, shhh, crash!*
This is it -
the world is at an end,
but as I am faced with this inevitable outcome
I stop and think!
All of *our* actions have resulted in
a world where no one cares,
a world where no one thinks,
a world where no one smiles.
This is our world
and our world is at an end.

Joshua Cerefice (13)
Blessed Edward Jones Catholic High School, Rhyl

Poverty

Homeless and poor
Very little food or water
People all over the world
No supply of clean water
Make poverty history!

Sam Pimley-Jones (13)
Blessed Edward Jones Catholic High School, Rhyl

The World Today

The TV on full-blast,
Radio switched on,
People on the sofa drinking all day long.
The man in the corner
On the PC,
The man on the phone
Speaking so loud.
That's the world inside;
Bright and loud!

Outside of the house
There are leaves on the ground.
Litter mixed in too.
Cars going *vroom*.
But apart from that
It's quiet and dark.

What's happening to the world?
Where's the nature gone?
People dying from pollution,
Animals being hunted
By us today.

What are we going to do?
Let it go rotten
Or shall we turn
It around and fix
It today?

Get the green grass back!
Pick up the litter!
Turn down the TV
And get off the phone!
Let's change the world
Today!

Andrew Greenow (12)
Blessed Edward Jones Catholic High School, Rhyl

Our Responsibility

The giant panda is becoming extinct
with nothing to eat and nothing to chew.
They only eat one thing
and that is bamboo.
The panda's nearly gone -
so it's up to you.

People are sighing.
People are crying.
People are dying.
Nothing to eat
nowhere to sleep
and nothing to wear.
What are we doing
to all of you out there?

Joel Jones (13)
Blessed Edward Jones Catholic High School, Rhyl

The World

Leave our animals alone
You're destroying their home
We want our animals to stay
Go, please, go away!

Recycle, recycle, recycle
We could make a bicycle
So turn off the lights and save
And the world won't go to the grave

That's it from me
It's time to see
Whether we can make the world a better place
And accept one another's race.

Jade Byrne (13)
Blessed Edward Jones Catholic High School, Rhyl

No Medal Of Honour

Soldiers here,
Soldiers there.
Their brave souls in despair.
The ground was brown sand,
Now it's red, as red as a Roman theatre.
They go in - two out of the platoon will survive.
The medal of honour is no medal to them.
Their medal is their family, especially the children.

Wives here.
Wives there.
Their waiting souls are in despair.
Their minds were filled with laughter,
Now they're filled with fear.
A memory is all they've got.
They want their husbands back.
Some know
They will never return.
The children wait.

Alexander Rowan (12)
Blessed Edward Jones Catholic High School, Rhyl

War

     W hy
fe A r
  w R ong!

Guns firing,
Bombs blowing,
Dead men lying in the dirt,
Many people gone,
Because of those terrifying bombs,
And now people are always on *red* alert.

Luke Wandless (13)
Blessed Edward Jones Catholic High School, Rhyl

I Was There

Bombs dropping,
Guns firing,
I was there! I saw it all!

Children screaming,
Homeless families,
I was there! I saw it all!

Scared children,
Terrifying noises,
I was there! I heard it all!

Wounded soldiers,
Nobody felt safe,
I was there! I felt it all!

Emily Howell-Smith (12)
Blessed Edward Jones Catholic High School, Rhyl

Racism

Being cruel to appearance
Because of colour
Making people feel different
Because of race
Filling people with shame and fear
Because of their nation
There can be a cure
There will be a cure
For racism.

Liam Sean Bateman (13)
Blessed Edward Jones Catholic High School, Rhyl

Polar Bear

Oh polar bear, oh polar bear, where art thou polar bear?
I look for you and you are nowhere.
You're disappearing.
Here and there people are hunting for your hair.
(Pretty coats and furry hats).
People think that that's that,
But they don't know what really matters.
You are leaving one by one.
It's you that matters,
Not a hat!

Shea McCarney (12)
Blessed Edward Jones Catholic High School, Rhyl

Braveheart War

War, why is war a tragedy?
Why do people die?
Why do people fight? To die?
For pride, for love, for freedom?

Once a very peaceful place,
Full of love and laughter,
Now a very desolate place,
Full of blood and death.
Maybe you should think again
And try to end it *now!*

Ryan Neary-Clarke (12)
Blessed Edward Jones Catholic High School, Rhyl

Am I A Nobody?

I am a nobody,
I have nothing,
That's what the people say
When they walk past me in the streets.

I'm a nobody,
I have no siblings, no parents,
They went to Heaven.
No family have I.

I see people some days,
Both younger and older than me,
They have everything,
Friends, family, love and hope.
I am alone.

I often wish I was a child with a family and love.
I want someone to love me,
I want someone to be with me,
But I'm scared that they'll laugh
Because I know I am nobody.

Kayleigh Woodward (13)
Blessed Edward Jones Catholic High School, Rhyl

Poverty

People dying every day
of disease such as HIV and AIDS.
In acute pain and stricken by starvation.
So many children suffering so young.
Dying from the ages of five to ten.
The truth hurts, we, the lucky people.
Yes it does!
Why does it?
Why?

Laura Hollinworth (13)
Blessed Edward Jones Catholic High School, Rhyl

Global Warming

A tourist approached me and said, 'What is global warming?'
I said, 'It is a race against time.'
Bitter icebergs are melting,
Useless gases are being pushed into the ozone layer.
The solution is - clean up your act,
Cycle to work,
More recycling,
The more energy we save
The ozone layer and the atmosphere will be fixed.

Sean Smith (15)
Brooke School, Rugby

Recycling

R ecycle, reuse, reduce
E lectrical appliances that don't work
C ardboard
Y oghurt pots
C lothes
L ower the amount of litter to save
E nergy.

Kieran English (16)
Brooke School, Rugby

Litter

L itter, put it in the bin
I n the bin it must go
T idy up our country
T idy up the world
E co-friendly
R ecycle your rubbish.

Lucy Cave
Brooke School, Rugby

Pollution

P lastic bags are dangerous to the world
O il spills, put something on it if you spill oil
L itter causes pollution
L itter is dangerous to the world
U nderstand the danger
T idy up the planet
I recycle newspapers
O il is making the Earth hot
N o! Leave your car at home.

Michael McKinney (15)
Brooke School, Rugby

Rubbish

R ubbish rubbish, what a mess
U gly and unnecessary
B irds swooping, looking for food
B ags, bottles, cans, paper, plastic, lying everywhere
I nsects buzzing greedily above heaps of waste
S mells of rotten food and dirt and dust
H elp us, *recycle* all you can!

Mickey White & David Pyle (14)
Brooke School, Rugby

Recycle

R ecycle, recycle, reuse, reduce.
E xtinction of animals.
C FCs. CO_2 (carbon dioxide), clothes, compost.
Y ou can help.
C arbon footprints, cutting down trees, cardboard.
L andfill, litter, less trees, less oxygen.
E nergy.

Samuel Cliffe (15)
Brooke School, Rugby

Volcano

D ying trees and flowers
E verything set on fire
S moke makes us cough, I nearly pass out
T ragedy
R olling lava
U ntidy
C overing the land
T otal devastation
I njured animals running
O ver hot ashes
N othing but ash left!

Xenon Bourne, Daniel Barford & Sergio Skyba-Lewin (14)
Brooke School, Rugby

Stop The Rubbish

Smelly and stinky
Yucky and sticky
Make sure all your rubbish
Goes straight into the bin

People are lazy
Throwing glass around
Children and animals
Get cuts and scars.

Bradley Hughes (13)
Brooke School, Rugby

To War

A rmed forces fighting for their country
R escue people in danger
M assacre lots of people
Y oung soldiers sent to war.

Sam Wilkins (13)
Brooke School, Rugby

Save Our Earth

S top the damage
A lways be alert
V alue the environment
E veryone can make a difference

O nly one world, don't spoil it
U nite together
R ecycle your rubbish

E arth is in danger
A sk how you can help
R egenerate the planet
T hink of polar bears
H urry, before it's too late!

Class S3
Brooke School, Rugby

Homeless People

Sitting on the street, begging for money
Waiting to go back to my cardboard box
In the back of the alley is where I live
I have to look into your house every night
I wish I had a house like yours.

Kyle Defty (12)
Brooke School, Rugby

Save The Rhinos

What happend to all the rhinos?
Stop the hunting.
Leave them alone.
We mustn't lose the rhinos.

Ryan O'Keeffe (12)
Brooke School, Rugby

How Can We Stop Climate Change?

Climate change is affecting our world,
Our lives and the lovely animals on Earth.

Caused by humans
Working in industrial places.
Power stations, car factories
All making pollution.

We have one chance,
We can make a big difference to the world.
Turn the temperature down a degree!

Climate change must stop
And we can stop it now!

Joel Mearns (13)
Brooke School, Rugby

Save Planet Earth

You've heard it all before,
On the news, in books and at school,
About the violence of war.
How we treat animals, so harsh and cruel.
How we cut down trees for our selfish needs.
How we pollute the sea and the air.
By doing all this we're destroying the planet and its breeds.
We need to stop *now* and start to care,
Before it's too late.

Recycle and save energy for what it's worth,
Take action and join the debate,
To save our home, Planet Earth.

Sophie Arthur (15)
Campion School, Leamington Spa

Make The Future Green

The dustbins are overflowing,
The countryside is going,
Pollution in the sea and air.
Litter is everywhere!

The world is falling, going down.
People look on with a frown.
Our world's resources going fast,
Oh how we long for the good, green past.

We feel the Earth is heating up,
The ozone layer blowing up,
Global warming back again.
Our planet will soon be gone.

But we can help bring back the past -
Recycle cans, bottles and jars.
Ditch your cars, walk or bike
See what difference we can make.

Jessica Faulkner (12)
Chipping Campden School, Chipping Campden

No Place To Go

A cushion on the street,
No shoes on your feet,
No food, no cash,
Just eating scraps from trash.

I wish I had a mum and dad,
I'm not that bad,
What have I done wrong?
These days feel really long.

I beg for help,
I'll scream and I'll yelp,
Give me a home,
I don't want to roam!

Leah James (12)
Chipping Campden School, Chipping Campden

Saving The World

The world is on its way out
And that is without a doubt
The sun is becoming brighter
And the nights are getting lighter

We're losing all our seasons
And the weather is a mess
There are many reasons
Most of which you can guess

We need to think more carefully
About how much we throw
Plastic, glass and paper
Can be recycled, as we know

We need to make some changes
We need to think it through
We can all help to save the world
But there's so much left to do!

Kelsey Noonan (13)
Cyfarthfa High School, Merthyr Tydfil

Save The World

We need to be eco-friendly to nature and mankind,
So before you ruin the planet think of all the damage you do
And leave behind with the spray of a can and sprinkle of ash,
This is the type of thing that won't stop the world from choking.

Trees will stop growing, the sun will stop shining,
The seasons will end, and if you let the world get to this stage,
It will be impossible to mend.

Think of others, for the future to come.
Remember our lives have only just begun.
So try your best, just do your part,
Trust me you'll be thankful,
You must have a place for the environment in your heart.

Olivia Katie Jones (13)
Cyfarthfa High School, Merthyr Tydfil

Earth's Enemy

Nowhere to run
From the degrading sun,
No laughter and fun,
What harm have we done?

Our planet is falling,
Into darkness and depths we are crawling,
Because of global warming,
The sun's rays are swarming.

Earth is coming apart at the seam.
Fighting through every extreme,
UV rays are burning,
Why isn't the human race learning?

Like a hole ripped in the surface,
It's such a disgrace,
Everyone gather and say a prayer,
There's nothing to do but stop and stare.

From the heat,
Rising around our feet,
Destruction is not the answer,
Why give us cancer?

Amy Alex Hoyland (13)
Cyfarthfa High School, Merthyr Tydfil

The Panda

The panda is a magnificent creature,
Black and white is its best feature.
It lives in rainforests in Asia,
Eating bamboo is its fantasia.
What horror if pandas became extinct.
How to save them must become distinct.
Some pandas are bred in the zoo,
To make them last for me and you.

Jessica Thurloway (14)
Millais School, Horsham

Eye Of The Tiger

I'm looking down and now I know,
The dangers of humans.
They warm the globe
And destroy our homes,
They just don't seem to care.

I thought I liked them,
They liked me
And now I know
The truth behind
All that silly nonsense.

You won't understand
Unless you're one of us,
How hard life
Can really be.
It's truly very tough.

I'm orange and black,
As I'm sure you will know,
I'm killed for my fur,
This I do not deserve.

I am endangered,
Because of humans.
They just don't seem to care.

Emily Bailey (14)
Millais School, Horsham

What Will Become Of It?

I watch the river flow as I sit,
If we carry on we will just pollute it.

The fields will turn from green to brown,
Smoke will rise above the town.

Global warming in the atmosphere,
You can tell humans lived here.

Alisha Elliott (14)
Millais School, Horsham

Puddles Of Tears

As the rain falls
I sit all alone,
listen to the calls
from someone's phone.
They're not for me,
but it makes me feel better,
I'm sitting by a tree,
getting wetter and wetter.

I see my mates
walk home from school.
They have a home,
I think they're cool.
I wonder what it's like,
like to be them,
with friends and family and food,
I don't have any of them.

As people walk past
I lay there in hope,
but no one will help me,
they won't throw me a rope.
I wonder what it's like,
like to be loved,
by a friend that cares,
so I wouldn't get shoved.

That's the whole reason
I lie in the street.
My parents don't love me,
they kick, punch and beat.

Jasmine Hewitt (14)
Millais School, Horsham

The Hunters

I just sit in there,
In my little cage,
My face fixed on him,
Ready to jump out in rage.

I pick myself up,
My eyes open wide,
I want to stretch out,
I did, I tried.

My foot on the floor,
In the runner of the tram,
Broken, no doubt,
Sad as I am.

My gnashing teeth,
My large, evil eyes,
My scary, loud roar,
These are the lies.

Wild as I am,
So patient and tame,
I've been hunted down,
For something so lame.

Catherine Lucey (14)
Millais School, Horsham

Global Warming

Global warming, the emotion I felt
Watching the great ice caps melt.

Polar bears and animals left in fear
And in danger of no longer living here.

Whilst humans keep electricals off and on,
When did this world become so wrong?

We just can't do nothing, we can't just sit,
We have got to do something before we pollute it!

Helen Towers (14)
Millais School, Horsham

Untitled

I once lived in a tree,
I was once free,
But then they got me.

They tore me apart
And ripped out my heart,
They didn't care, they laughed.

They put my skin on,
What a con!
They sold my fat to make jelly bonbon.

No one cares,
All they want is something to wear.

Lily Olden (13)
Millais School, Horsham

Segregation

Segregation - it needs to come to an end.
Discrimination - a bad message to send.

All the colours - to meet and stay.
Prejudice - never to say.

Good and evil - no longer to be
In our lives - for eternity.

We should learn that now and forever,
Black and white should be together.

Honor Amy Turpin (12)
Moreton Hall, Oswestry

Dear Mr President

Dear Mr President,
Have you seen what has been going on for all these years?
The ice caps are melting,
Poor little polar bears getting drowned at the bottom of the sea.
Countries are flooding,
People are homeless, starving and cold.
Do you realise what is going on?
We are ruining the world!
Why do you let this happen?
You have the power to tell the world.

Lauren Howe (13)
Moreton Hall, Oswestry

Animals

Animals are becoming extinct
Because of past caring people.
Trees are getting chopped right down
But don't forget they are homes too.
The wonderful animals in our cruel world
Are disappearing in a blink.
In our days people forget to think.
Would you really like it if they knocked your home down?
So in future do something simple which costs nothing
Just stop and think,
To stop animals being extinct
Until we all know it's gone past the limit.

Darian Duggan (12)
Nantyglo Comprehensive School, Nantyglo

A War Of Sin

On this battlefield we fight to win,
Though we are committing sin,
They aim their guns,
We raise our swords,
We pierce their lungs,
They snap our spinal cords.
He bares the crown of thorns,
He can hear his mother's mourns,
It is now her time to cry,
She sees her son slowly die,
As I fight in this war I pray I'm forgiven,
For all the sins I've just committed.
I lie in the blood of a sinner,
I guess I'm not a winner,
I promised my husband, I promised my child,
I would come back to see them smile.
My life flashes before my eyes,
Will I see Lucifer for all my lies?
Or am I forgiven for saving lives?
I pray at the golden gate,
All I'm left to do is wait,
'He died for all our sin!'
'I beg you now my Lord, let me in!'

Rebecca Koash (13)
Nantyglo Comprehensive School, Nantyglo

War

War is awful
All the shooting
Rage and death
Friend or foe
All over land
Eventually we will stop and live in peace.

Joshua Griffiths (11)
Nantyglo Comprehensive School, Nantyglo

Animals And Extinction

Animals are dying,
Some are even trying.
Animals are gone,
This is so wrong.

We fight for these animals
We fight very hard.
For these animals to live
So they are not gone.

Animals should have a happy life,
Instead of being killed with a knife.
Animals shouldn't be bait,
Or otherwise it will be too late.
Animals shouldn't be locked in a cage,
Or they will be full of rage.

Animals are dying,
Some are even trying.
Animals are nearly gone,
This is so wrong.

Kirsty Allison (13)
Nantyglo Comprehensive School, Nantyglo

Animals

A nimals are becoming extinct.
N ow people are starting to help.
I t is getting dangerous.
M ost animals are getting killed.
A frican people are hunting them.
L et them live in freedom.
S top hunting, killing and trapping animals.

Lewis Hodges (12)
Nantyglo Comprehensive School, Nantyglo

Rainforests

Rainforests are so beautiful,
Why chop them away?
That's really ungrateful,
Animals want to stay.
That's why animals are becoming extinct
Throwing away their habitats
Wildlife will be gone in a blink
Scaring poor bats and rats.

Animals make you feel loved,
Just like Noah's ark and the dove.
We are animals so how would you feel?
If bears and rabbits came and knocked down our homes?
Wildlife and trees are real so why knock down their homes?
Help us campaign to stop rainforests being thrown away
And have the feeling of life and beauty, coming our way.

Hope Ayeisha Victoria Meek (12)
Nantyglo Comprehensive School, Nantyglo

Being Homeless

Being homeless isn't pleasant
I just wish someone could buy me a present
I should have a happy life
Instead of people trying to stab me with a knife.

I am alone with no one to hold
In the night it sure is cold
I have no money, food or drink,
All I do is sit and think.

I have dirty hair
Not even money to go in the fair
I wish I could have a home
And not be left alone.

Phoebe Bridge (12)
Nantyglo Comprehensive School, Nantyglo

Extinction Of Animals

Animals are extinct, every second that we blink
It is because of the hunters who kill.
For those animals cannot win. This is not fair,
The animals they dare to kill, to fight, to live for the life they have.

Animals are kind, they are fearless. Though the hunters think
                            they are not
The animal thinks of their family, their friends, their lives.
This killing is not acceptable.
It will not be forgiven!

We blink, they are gone, all that's left is the song of their voice,
                            of their nature.
In the dark, in the night, the hunters kill, it is scary, it is cruel.
Do not let them do this!

Extinction is wrong, the animals are gone
Do not be sad for their lives
Let them live and give us five.

Tori Williams (12)
Nantyglo Comprehensive School, Nantyglo

Don't Take The Car

Don't take the car
If the journey isn't far
Just hop on your bike
And pedal where you like

But if you take the car
On a journey that's not far
It gives off all that gas
So the planet doesn't last

So please don't take the car
When the journey isn't far
Please take the bike
It's transport that the planet likes.

Rhys Evans (12)
Nantyglo Comprehensive School, Nantyglo

Wah, Wah

Wah, wah go the sirens in the night
As the children and adults cry in fright

Boom, boom as the bombs fall
Houses being destroyed which didn't go so well

Bang, bang go the guns in the night
Why should people die by a bullet or even a knife?

Wah, wah as the sirens call the all clear
Children and adults climbing out of bomb shells in shock and fear.

Choo, choo goes the train for the young
As they're travelling to Wales to avoid the bullet of a gun.

Wah, wah cry the children in the train
Being separated from their parents must be the ultimate pain.

Choo, choo the train stops
The children step out of the train, tears running down faces from fear
and shock.

Whoa, whoa as the children look at this place where there is green
grass, sheep and trees.
The children standing there with shock and amazement as they're
trembling at the knees.

Morgan Jenkins (13)
Nantyglo Comprehensive School, Nantyglo

The Minstrels Of War

Bombs falling, sirens blaring,
Dead corpses hitting the floor,
All of these are the instruments,
Of the minstrels of war.

Guns shooting, buildings crashing,
Armed men booting down the door,
All of these are the instruments,
Of the minstrels of war.

Cars exploding, missiles zooming,
Devastation not heard of before
All of these are the instruments,
Of the minstrels of war.

Soldiers rushing, civilians running,
Though all these things I do deplore,
All of these are the instruments,
Of the minstrels of war.

Connor Griffiths (13)
Nantyglo Comprehensive School, Nantyglo

Reduce, Reuse And Recycle

There was a young man called Kyle,
Who went the extra mile,
To recycle his waste -
He hurried in haste,
Down to the recycle pile.

Kyle Winterbottom (20)
Pengwern Residential College, Rhyl

Help!

Help the environment to win,
Put it in the recycling bin.
Cans of pop, glass and card,
Be environmentally friendly it's not hard!

Teresa Walley & Diane Lee (17)
Pengwern Residential College, Rhyl

Polar Bears

In a cold white place,
Where the polar bears live,
White furry coats,
Big tall giants.
The ice is cracking,
The ice is melting,
The ice is crumbling,
Into the ocean.
Where will they live
When the ice has gone?

Lewis Berry (15)
Round Oak School, Warwick

Eco-Poem

The polar bears are dying
Lying there on the floor.
The penguins are squawking
Because their children are dead.
There are lights being left on
And it is wasting energy!
Compost is good so put your scraps in there!
What is the point in driving to your local shop?

Jack Moran (11)
Tenbury High School, Tenbury Wells

Eco World

Our world is being damaged,
Animals will be extinct,
We all need to go green.

To protect our world we need to recycle
You should recycle plastic bags
Or use a compost bin.

To preserve our world we need to stop pollution
You should use public transport
To stop gases from your car.

Zoe Leadbetter (12)
Tenbury High School, Tenbury Wells

The Eco-Code

Pick up your filthy litter and put it in the bin
Walk or cycle to save pollution from cars,
Turn your heating down and wear a jumper
Use a compost bin to put scrap, wasted food into.
Stop cutting trees down.
Pick up or reuse plastic bags,
Animals can die or be harmed by litter
Stop global warming!

Chloe Gittins (12)
Tenbury High School, Tenbury Wells

Eco Poem

Tick-tock we're running out of luck,
Tick-tock we need to stop.
Right now the Earth is breathing
So take a bus or a train,
To save the Earth from all this pain.
So tick-tock please stop.

Alice Withers (12)
Tenbury High School, Tenbury Wells

Green World

G reed cutting down the rainforest
R ecycle to conserve the Earth's resources
E ngines destroying the ozone
E nergy trying to be preserved
N ever the wildlife is safe.

W herever the trees will be safe and survive
O r the ice caps will melt
R ecycle plastic, paper and glistening metal
L orries and cars polluting the skies
D eath will come if all this continues.

Martin Bailey (12)
Tenbury High School, Tenbury Wells

Eco Poem

R euse energy, don't waste it.
E xtinction is happening all around the world.
C an you cycle or walk to places?
Y ou can change the world.
C an you please, please recycle
L ots of people recycle can you?
E co outgoing world please.

Anthony Cook (11)
Tenbury High School, Tenbury Wells

Lonely

Oil laps against the shore
A lonely crab
Trundling over debris
Carelessness caused the spill
The price paid by animals
Suffering for man's greed.

Hannah Hopkinson (13)
Tenbury High School, Tenbury Wells

Eco Poem

G lobal warming is going to happen,
R ecycling may save the Earth,
E xtinction to some animals
E nergy should be saved,
N ever pollute the Earth.

E co will save the Earth,
A nimals should be saved,
R ecycle for the Earth,
T he ice caps are melting,
H eating should be saved when you don't need it.

Tommy Village (11)
Tenbury High School, Tenbury Wells

Out Of My Window

The air turns to mist,
I open my window,
Air,
The rattling of plastic bags,
Like a room full of crying babies,
I watch in horror,
The world is a fireball,
Burning to nothing.

Alice Waite (13)
Tenbury High School, Tenbury Wells

The Crab

The crab stood on his own
Surrounded by oil
Abandoned in a different world
Threatened
The crab
A digger pulled itself through the dark
A current of sticky sludge.

Lucas Tisdale (13)
Tenbury High School, Tenbury Wells

Eco Poem

Greenhouse gases are polluting the world.
Litter is killing wildlife such as sea turtles, fish and lots more.
Only a little thinking and we can stop this.
Bike, walk or use public transport to reduce the pollution
All houses should have solar panels.
Lighting, TVs, game consoles and any other electricals
Should be turned off when not in use.
Washing machines should be put on 30°C.
All people should be trying to help.
Right now we need to stop and think,
More things should be recycled and more people should recycle.
It is super to recycle
Now is the time we can stop this
Gases from factories are polluting the world.

Georgie Bufton (11)
Tenbury High School, Tenbury Wells

Eco Poem

As the world heats up
Global warming is a major factor
Penguins, polar bears and other innocent animals are being killed.
Try and stop this
Recycling is a good idea
Reusing different materials
So the wastelands don't get bigger
To improve this situation
Keep the washing machines at 30°C
Cycling to school, not by car.
To prevent pollution and dense smog
If the world is going to stay longer
The beautiful rainforest and tremendous wildlife have to be protected!

Joe Webb (12)
Tenbury High School, Tenbury Wells

Homelessness - You And I

You get a warm house and warm bed,
I get a cardboard box on a street corner.
You get safety and support from your family,
I get drunks walking past and spitting on my feet.
You can choose if you want to get involved with the police,
I am picked up by them every morning and get thrown back out
at night.

You can be clean and wash every day,
I have rats scuttling over my feet and a shower on a rainy day.
I feel something isn't right here, do you?

Amy Byers (12)
Tenbury High School, Tenbury Wells

Eco Poem

Gases from fuming factories fill the air with poison pollution.
The old, crumbling factory pumps deathly black smoke into the air.
Puffs of smoke rise higher and higher.
Creating the ozone layer, making it thicker and thicker, deadlier
and deadlier,
Slowly killing the world . . .

Jasmine Bibby (12)
Tenbury High School, Tenbury Wells

My Global Warming Poem

G lobal warming kills us and animals around us.
R euse plastic bags, don't drop them on the floor.
E veryone working together to make the world a better place
E ven we can die from global warming so stop now.
N ever drop litter on the floor, put it in bins close by.

Leanne Potter (12)
Tenbury High School, Tenbury Wells

Eco Poem

Running along the bare ground,
Tripping on tree stumps,
Anxiously looking around
I swear there were trees here,
But now the ground I'm running on,
Seems completely clear
Apart from a mess
Of branches and dying animals,
Lying in distress.
They took all our trees away
Why would they do that?
I'll have nowhere to live,
For yet another day
No trees for me to climb up
Just trees to make me trip up.
Who would do this to us?

Georgie Clark (12)
Tenbury High School, Tenbury Wells

My Eco Poem!

The gases kill the Earth,
Is that all it is worth?
Does it matter if people die?
Can we stop it, can we try?
Why not turn the heating down?
To use for any other town.
Animals should have a chance to live,
Is death the only thing people give?
There's no excuses, no room to dither,
People shouldn't pollute every river.
If you alone, even worry or care,
Watch over this world that we all have to share.

Emma Nicholls (12)
Tenbury High School, Tenbury Wells

War

The beast of war
The force of Mars
They muster their armies,
And start the charge.

A sea of devils,
Enriched by fire,
Nothing can extinguish
The bane of desire.

And left in the sorrow,
That follows war's wake,
Alone in the field,
A country's dark fate.

So war has no reason,
No reasons to doubt,
Just lies and conspiracy,
And death all about.

James Lloyd (14)
Tenbury High School, Tenbury Wells

Global Warming

G ases in the air!
L ack of natural trees.
O il in the sea!
B oiling sun melts the ice.
A ir becoming carbon dioxide.
L itter on the floor.

W ildlife less in numbers!
A fraid it will flood.
R ecycle as much as you can.
M ore and more water from the ice!
L I ghting can be reduced.
N ature being destroyed!
G lobal warming is a critical thing!

Richard Strawford (12)
Tenbury High School, Tenbury Wells

Pollution

Pollution, pollution lurks everywhere,
It's getting less and less rare.
Pollution is melting all of the ice,
So it's not really nice.
Using cars, lorries and aeroplanes,
Every time pollution gains,
This problem is bigger and greater,
So don't wait till later!
You can reduce it in many ways,
Not sitting to have a laze.
Run or bike,
Or you can hike.
All of this can reduce,
And save animals like the moose,
So have some fun and walk
It's a great way to have a talk.
Only we can save the environment
Because if not pollution will dent,
Every little bit can stop it,
Even though it might take us a bit.

Jordan Powell (12)
Tenbury High School, Tenbury Wells

Eco-Catastrophe

Nuclear stations pump out fatal gases,
Killing all the green grass.
Global warming melts ice caps,
And extinction is all around.

Litter scattered everywhere,
Choking all of the scenery around.

There are ways to stop all of these things,
All of the rubbish, everything.

But still we carry on destroying this world,
And if we do we will all suffer!

David Parsons (12)
Tenbury High School, Tenbury Wells

Who Will Find The World Its Feet?

I know I am not perfect
Believe me, I'm no saint,
But I do detect our one defect
Anxiety is late.

The trees fall like our soldiers,
A thousand wounds a day.
They're not as bold as people told us -
They still just chop away.

One poem can't change political mess,
I'll not pretend it can.
If the hypocritical took the blame a little,
The world would go to plan.

Prevent this pollution,
Cease this disease,
Just grab a bike (ditch the cab)
Who says we're all obese?

But do it now - not next week,
If you forget, you'll just regret,
That you too did not seek,
A way to find the world its feet.

Natalie Nicholls-Lamb (15)
Tenbury High School, Tenbury Wells

Litter Guilt

Just think when you feel dim,
Why couldn't you have put that packet in the bin?
It's just going to lie there,
Making those animals so, so rare.
What had those animals ever done
To get trapped whilst you just run?
You are to blame,
This isn't a game.
Sort it out,
Don't feel the doubt.

Christie James (12)
Tenbury High School, Tenbury Wells

Cease Evil Global Warming!

Wrap up in layers of clothes,
Don't turn the heating on!
Turn it down or even off to save using all the oils.
Use public transport - taxis and trains,
Walking or cycling might be a change.
Don't drop wrappers, gum or bags,
Put them in a bin to save all animals.
Use more eco oils and gases.
Put an end to cutting down so many trees,
Use both sides of paper.
Stop and reflect on that one word
Green!

Bethan Dennis (12)
Tenbury High School, Tenbury Wells

Landfills

Noisy, polluted,
A very unpleasant place.
Diggers are giants eating away the dirt,
Bulldozers are like car crushes
Crushing all the waste,
Recycle, reuse,
Be kind to our planet that you are destroying.
Otherwise the light of our sun will be blown out like a fuse.

Kate Yarnold (12)
Tenbury High School, Tenbury Wells

The World

People killing, people dying.
Children hurting, you see them crying.

Life destroyers, confidence takers,
The world is hard-hearted, relationship breakers.

Carla Dallow (13)
Tenbury High School, Tenbury Wells

Wasted Energy

Energy is being wasted, we are coming to an end,
Please don't do any more you're driving me around the bend.

Help me save the world otherwise you'll die.
Look, look up there, there in the sky.

Pollution is killing us, choking us to death.
Shutting us down forever.

Don't sit watching TV, wasting your life and drinking tea.

Help, help me! We can rule supreme, eliminate pollution and make
this world clean.

Together we can make a difference.
And do this sinking battleship proud.
You can stand up, in front of all this crowd.

Don't delay, have your say, send our message round.

Declan Morbey (11)
Tenbury High School, Tenbury Wells

Rainforest

R aindrops, raindrops coming down fast makes the forest last
and last.
A nimals always wandering around some even live under the ground.
I nsects, bugs everywhere can even give you quite a scare.
N ights in the forest can be so dark, it is so quiet you can't hear
a bark.
F rog, pig, wild snakes roam around the forest lakes.
O range, blue, yellow, green are the colours that are seen.
R ich green leaves needed for food puts the animals in a good mood.
E legant birds sitting on their nests wait for their egg to hatch
like the rest.
S ky-high trees so thick and tall helps the nest not to fall.
T rickling streams like a refreshing pool, makes the forest feel so cool.

Katherine Whistance (12)
Tenbury High School, Tenbury Wells

Polar Bear Extinction

Melting ice in the Atlantic,
Killing the innocent species,
Nothing for them to stand on,
Drown, their only option.
Obviously the polar bear,
Is fascinating enough,
Without being spread across the news,
As they are no more.
If only people would listen,
To their plea to the world,
Then maybe, just maybe,
They *will* stay on this astounding Earth.

Scott Dallow (12)
Tenbury High School, Tenbury Wells

Recycle

R   ecycle
E   verything you can
Be C   ause we need to help save the Earth
Y   ou
C   an make a difference
L   ove
E   arth and recycle.

Ben Jordan (12)
Tenbury High School, Tenbury Wells

War - Haiku

War destroys the world
Angry soldiers fighting on
Embracing their death.

Ellie Mapp (12)
Tenbury High School, Tenbury Wells

Why Does No One Care?

Why does no one care
About the Earth that we all share?
By just a small walk a day,
Our lovely Earth will be here to stay!

Animals are dying every day
As the rainforest gets hacked away;
Do people like to cause this distress,
Ruining homes and creating mess?

Do you need that electric light?
I think not until the night.
Would you like us all to die?
If not then please help us try!

Tara Nicholls (12)
Tenbury High School, Tenbury Wells

Animals And Extinction

We all start crying
When we don't see birds flying.
Sadness fills the air
When we don't see the bear.
When the lion went insane
He lost his mane
We are the killers here
So stop it now!

Amy Miles (12)
Tenbury High School, Tenbury Wells

Rainforest - Haiku

Silence is broken
When the destroyers arrive,
Everything now dies.

Jonquil Ives (13)
Tenbury High School, Tenbury Wells

Eco Poem!

Sea turtles are dying you say!
Think about it . . .
Polar bears are leaving you say!
Think about it . . .
Why do our sea turtles die you ask?
Think about it . . .
Our plastic bags fool them
Think about it . . .
How can we help you ask?
Think about it . . .
What about recycling you say!
Think about it . . .
Turn electricity off to cool the air you say,
Think about it . . .
That will stop the ice caps melting you say,
Stop thinking, start doing.

Bethany Hayward (12)
Tenbury High School, Tenbury Wells

A Rainforest

Trees wave,
Rivers glaze,
Animals all around,

Some skuttering,
Others muttering,
Every single sound,

Sun shining,
Wind whining,
Colour fills the sky,

Every aspect of happiness
And we all ask why.

Clare Kerby (13)
Tenbury High School, Tenbury Wells

Homeless

Cold fingers, cold toes,
Don't really have a home,
Begs along the side of roads,
Dark places no one goes,
Dodgy toilets might be someone's home,
Clothes that usually last weeks,
And with us we change to sleep,
Find hats to keep them warm,
People walking quickly past,
Murmuring insults and faults,
Of that person sitting there,
In dirty ruffled clothes,
But if you think . . .
We're all humans
Just like you and me
They might have a great personality!

Jess Sanders (12)
Tenbury High School, Tenbury Wells

Extinction

Sadness and darkness fill the air,
As the tiger and lion lose their lives,
And the fish are polluted by oil,
We are the killers here.

The weather hit the bees,
Because of global warming,
We pollute and litter,
We are the killers here.

The panda baby loses its mum,
For that gun he dies too,
We never lived to see the dodo,
We can make a difference,
For the sake of animal welfare!

Francesca Jones (13)
Tenbury High School, Tenbury Wells

Eco-World

The ice caps are melting
His trucks are polluting
Energy is being wasted
Extinction of our animals
Nothing is being done
Very valuable things are going
Instead of staying
Recycle your litter
Or reuse peelings
Much can be done
Extinction shouldn't happen
Never cut down trees
Trees are here to help us.

Dan Pitt (11)
Tenbury High School, Tenbury Wells

Eco Poem

G lobal warming, remember this and recycle
R ecycle, your drinks cans and bottles
E nergy, turn things off when not in use
E co friendly, do things to help the world.
N ature, be kind to wildlife around you.

Lindsay Perkins (11)
Tenbury High School, Tenbury Wells

War Kennings

Life taking
Heart breaking
Noise making
Body aching
Death making
Legs shaking.

Jack Houchin (13)
Tenbury High School, Tenbury Wells

What If . . .

When I sit in a classroom,
Teacher talking on,
Never do I listen,
Much too busy worrying about things.
What if another tree gets cut down,
While she's babbling on?
What if the light in my room,
Destroys the whole world?
What if the ice caps melting,
Make the polar bears die?
What if the gas from my dad's car
Gets us all cooked alive?
My teacher says my writing's,
Much too small,
It's not my fault,
I want to save space,
So the trees don't fall.
What is she saying now?
We can save the world
Just turn the electric off,
If you're not using it.
Maybe I'll try that
Maybe you should too.
Help me concentrate in class
To know the world's in capable hands.

Anna Günther (12)
Tenbury High School, Tenbury Wells

Homeless Kennings

Alley taker,
Door stopper,
Coldness bringer,
Money loser,
Heart melter,
Home wanter,
Life begger.

Alice Pollard (13)
Tenbury High School, Tenbury Wells

War

War destroys the soul and mind,
Never will the dead arise,
This is no time for idleness because men will die,
There is no way to back away as the great horn does call,
And in the early hours of morn many people call,
Never will you go home ever quite the same again
War, it makes you distraught,
Makes you fear,
War destroys the soul and mind,
And stops life forever,
War tears the world apart,
And carries through all weather.

Death and toil,
Blood and sweat,
No it should not continue,
Although men still go,
Marching out to war,
Eager to slay the foe
Your country calls,
Never does it show until the death toll records.
Always fighting,
Never thinking.

War is the death bringer,
Life taker,
Grim reaper,
World destroyer,
Enemy maker,
Empire breaker,
Good men taker.

Callum Redding (12)
Tenbury High School, Tenbury Wells

Shall I Be An Angel, Daddy?

One day a father
To his little son
Told a sad story,
A heartbreaking one.
He took from an album
A photo and said,
'This is your mother,
But she's been long dead.

She was taken by famine
About five years ago.
Why poverty chose her,
We never shall know.

You, she has left me,
To cherish and love,
She is an angel, my child,
Up above.'

The boy in an instance
Drew close to his side
And these are the words
That he softly replied,

'Shall I be an angel, Daddy,
An angel in the sky?
Shall I wear the golden wings
And live in peace on high?
Shall I live forever and ever
With the angels fair?
If I go to Heaven,
Oh tell me, Daddy,
Will I see Mother there?'

Becky Tomkins Bevan (12)
Tenbury High School, Tenbury Wells

Beware! Beware!

Beware! Beware!
We are evil to our environment!
Animals are disappearing too quickly to stop!
Beware!

Beware! Beware!
Polar bears are disappearing because
There are few icebergs!
Beware!

Beware! Beware!
Our rainforests are
Being chopped down
Beware!

Beware! Beware!
The amount of cars are ruining the world!
The atmosphere is crumbling!
Beware!

Beware! Beware!
We are evil to our environment!
You can stop it!
Just beware!

Emily Holland (12)
Tenbury High School, Tenbury Wells

The Dragon

A dragon is roaming our planet,
He's vulgar, vicious and vile,
Leaving destruction in his path
And causing death all the while.

Devouring species to extinction,
Drinking the Earth's lifeblood,
Gnawing away at the coastlines,
Spreading poverty, disease and flood.

He's scorched a hole in the ozone layer,
With his fearsome, fiery breath,
The world smoulders under the sun's glare,
Dying a slow, painful death.

He's stomping all around the globe,
Looking to pick a fight,
Spreading hatred, conflict and war,
Costing many young lives.

This devastating dragon is evil,
Concocting his racist brew,
To make a barrier between white and black,
While feeding the poison to you.

The snarling monster sniggers,
As he tramples with his feet,
Overflowing landfill sites
And homeless children on the street.

He's gobbling up our rainforests,
Spewing pollution with his ghastly breath,
Slurping all Earth's precious oil,
Condemning mankind to its death.

But why are you quivering?
Why do you turn to flee?
You have the armour to conquer him,
We can beat him, you and me!

So grab your recycled metal sword,
Mount your non-polluting steed,
Put on your helmet of organic veg
And prepare to do the deed.

Switch off all the lights as you leave,
To fight the terrible foe,
Take your recycling in your 'Bag for Life',
To drop off as you go.

Hold your anti-racism shield,
Against the dragon's teeth
And confiscate all the aerosols,
From that ozone-stealing thief.

Plug his foul, polluting nostrils,
With energy-saving bulbs,
Stuff his slavering mouth with compost
And plant wind turbines on his nose.

Write across his scaly rump,
For the politicians to see,
'Hunting animals to extinction
And homelessness should never be!'

So band together dragon slayers,
Let's make this crisis end,
To stop that dragon from killing us,
We must all make amends.

Help to slay the dragon,
Before the Earth is through,
Save our world and stop the rot,
For the cause of this was *you!*

Isobel Goodman (12)
The Corbet School Technology College, Baschurch

Iceberg

I ce melting
C hilly weather
E xtreme climate
B ecoming an issue
E xtinction increasing
R ising water
G reen disappearing.

Amy Hayes (14)
The Cotswold School, Bourton-on-the-Water

Is This Really Our World?

Destruction, death and devastation,
Evil creates a war of the worlds.
Loneliness, isolation and desperation,
Evil earns all wealth out of selfishness.

Is this fair?

Poverty, illness, starvation,
Evil leaves countries to suffer.
Gas emissions, carbon footprints and pollution,
Evil takes no care of its home.

Is this green?

Racism, being different and separation,
Evil is determined to break races.
Selfishness, competing for wealth, desperation,
Evil leaves others to take pain for their happiness.

Is this how a world should be?
And who are these *evil*?
You decide!

Emilia McIntyre (13)
The Cotswold School, Bourton-on-the-Water

Warning

The number of homeless
polar bears is rising
at an alarming rate.

We like it when
it's hot
polar bears like it when it's not

Polar bears like to swim and play
but they don't like to
stay in water all day.

Charlotte Green (14)
The Cotswold School, Bourton-on-the-Water

Colour Of My Skin

Black or white
Or even striped?
We are all the same,
Whether red, green, yellow or grey!
Why the segregation?
Leaving them in the rain . . .
To fend for themselves.
No colour is better than another
And no brother would disrespect his mother.
So why in the world do we see no face?
We must look deeper than a simple race,
To see the wonderful people in the world,
Who could change our lives
And remain the same.
Equality is the key!
So see me for me!

Ruby Fenton (14)
The Cotswold School, Bourton-on-the-Water

Imagination Or Reality

Imagine living in fear
Imagine losing loved ones
Imagine losing your home and livelihood
Imagine having one meal a day - if that
Imagine no one caring
Imagine tanks roaring past
Imagine, imagine, imagine
Imagine this on a huge scale
This is not imagination, this is reality
Most have lost homes and livelihood
Most don't eat at all
No one cares about these poor people
This is reality!

Ben Glass (15)
The Cotswold School, Bourton-on-the-Water

Is This Peace?

Crying children, sitting alone,
Dreading their parents coming home.
Jumping and wincing at every sound,
Hiding in the corner, not wanting to be found.
Outside, a car engine suddenly stops,
Their parents have just returned from the shops.
When the key turns in the lock,
The frightened children freeze in shock.
A shuffle of footsteps, a rustle of bags,
The air changes to stale, smoked fags.
The children emerge, brave-faced and red,
The parents have already sent them to bed.
Can you imagine a life like this?
As you can see it's not all bliss,
Some poor children have this all day,
Do you think it is the right way?

Laura Martin (14)
The Cotswold School, Bourton-on-the-Water

Six Little Ducks

Brainless people walking around,
Dumping rubbish on the ground.
Killing wildlife and all its things,
Some ghastly things that will make you cringe.

Six little ducks, walking in two lines,
Walking behind each other as if they were blind.
You wouldn't believe it but they sure can peck,
But beer-can packaging is around their necks.

So please stop littering
And make this world less sickening.
Get the Earth in saving mode
And you could help change the globe.

Sophie Witt (13)
The Cotswold School, Bourton-on-the-Water

Help Me

I am sick
Empty faces turn towards me
Unfamiliar in my misery
On the seventh day I cannot move
I watch the sun rise
And it is no longer good
The warmth on my face merely a memory
Of what I am - lost

I am poor
Homeless. Helpless
Burned by a merciless sun
Crying, weeping
It was lost before I was born
Burned away to dirt and dust

I am fighting
Because now I am God
Angel of death
Flesh is my bread and blood my wine
My gun my cross
Bitter, boiling hatred

I am dying
Metal bites into me
Creaking, crying
I scream as I fall
And crash to the ground
Leafless, lifeless

I am wrong
Fine webs and nets of nerves
The pigment painted over me
Killing me
Because of me
My skin is wrong

I am sick
Burned by a merciless sun
Bitter, boiling hatred
Metal bites into me
They're killing me

You're killing me
I'm choking.

Tess Simpson (14)
The Cotswold School, Bourton-on-the-Water

War

Death, horror, stench,
Destruction of homes, lives and families.
Suffering children, massacres of towns,
Genocide of people.

Lines of massed infantry,
Armed to face certain death.

Bombs dropping everywhere,
The death toll is rising,
The polluting smoke
Of the tanks
Running over frightened soldiers.

Machine guns and rifles,
Firing down at their targets,
Indiscriminately,
Snipers killing
At random.

Officers screaming orders
At their men.
The frightening screams as the shells explode
Right on top of them.

Iain York (15)
The Cotswold School, Bourton-on-the-Water

Look At What Humans Have Done

Revving up the engine,
The man gets on his way,
To a busy, bustling airport
Only two minutes away.

Out of the Arctic whiteness
A huge shape appears,
Followed by her little ones,
Their journey will take years.

Stepping out of his 4X4,
The man lights a fag,
Unaware of the harm it will do,
He chucks a plastic bag.

Mother bear pads silently,
Over the thin, thin snow,
All around her home is melting,
Soon she'll have nowhere to go.

The man turns off his phone,
His laptop and his pager,
As he boards his long-haul flight
On its way to Nigeria.

Mother and cubs stare in awe,
At the water before them,
No ice can be seen for miles and miles,
All thanks to global warming.

Eating food from around the world,
The man smiles with glee;
He is going to be a millionaire,
Thanks to his oil company.

Hungrily licking their lips.
The cubs look up to their mum,
Seals are becoming scarce now,
They've been poached and now they're gone.

The man reaches Nigeria,
A black heart in his chest,
Uncaring to the harm he is doing,
He is like many in the west.

The bears struggle on and on,
As they will for years to come,
Combating the evils of climate change -
Look at what humans have done.

Sophie Mustoe (14)
The Cotswold School, Bourton-on-the-Water

Beyond The Poppies

Marching strong, tall and proud,
Horizon's blue, without a cloud,
Striding on past enemy lines,
Those who have fallen, left behind.

Smoke billowing straight ahead,
Grey and dim to scarlet-red.
Fire appears from between the trees,
Panicked men fall to their knees.

Heads fixed towards the skies,
The nightmare reflected in his eyes,
Cracked lips turn deep red,
All the confessions still left unsaid.

Men's dreams pierced by the flames,
Shudder of bombs and screaming of names.
Droning aeroplanes and the clattering guns,
Whispered names of all the loved ones.

Deafening sounds emerge violently,
Enemy snipers creeping silently.
All goes silent, but never for long,
We lost our men at the Battle of the Somme.

All that remains is an ocean of red,
Where injured soldiers were left for dead.
Field after field of poppies standing tall,
This beautiful landscape is where we fall.

Hannah Davis (14)
The Cotswold School, Bourton-on-the-Water

Alone

All on my own,
No one in sight,
I feel so alone,
In the dark, with no light.

I shiver from the cold,
Nothing to get me warmer,
With no one to hold,
Alone in my corner.

People walk by,
But they only stare,
Nobody says, 'Hi',
They don't even care.

What am I?
Homeless and alone.

Ellie James (15)
The Cotswold School, Bourton-on-the-Water

Poverty

(If this stupid poem can fix a home, I'll read it every day.)

Every three seconds
an African child dies.
This is the foundation
on which human evil lies.

Stop all the death,
cure the disease,
people can't just grow back,
not like plants or trees.

The next time you eat a meal
and think your life's unfair,
think about those children,
think of their despair.

Ryan Evans (15)
The Cotswold School, Bourton-on-the-Water

What's The Point Of Being Green?

A plastic bag at a supermarket,
A traffic jam in town,
A man with a chainsaw cutting down a tree
And litter on the ground.

Having a bath instead of a shower,
Not turning out the light,
An aeroplane leaving from a busy airport,
At the start of a long-haul flight.

All these things aren't eco-friendly,
But what's the point of being green?
It's so that future generations
Can see the wonders of the world that we have seen.

Rebecca Howard (14)
The Cotswold School, Bourton-on-the-Water

Global Warming

G rim future
L ost environment
O ld world
B ad future
A pocalypse
L arge amount of sun

W orrying for humans
A bomination of humans
R ural disaster
M ight have no hope
I t's only the beginning
N owhere to run
G oodbye world!

Jamie Goddard (13)
The Cotswold School, Bourton-on-the-Water

Captivity

Kept inside,
I'm losing my mind,
This is no way to live.

Separated from you
And the things that you do,
By the bars that keep me prisoner.

When people see me,
I wish that they could hear me,
Maybe then I'd be free.

As time goes by,
All I can do is lie
And hope that one day it will be over.

The nature of my life
Is not work, toil or strife,
But I am forced, simply, to be.

Or so it would seem,
To one who has never been
Able to go anywhere but here.

I'm bound up inside,
By my external hand,
Wondering what I did, to you.

Jack Howarth (15)
The Cotswold School, Bourton-on-the-Water

How To Fly? Said The Penguin

How to fly? said the penguin
pondering one day,
my home's being destroyed
and I don't have a say.

How to fly? said the penguin
it would just be nice
to fly away from this place
and escape the melting ice.

How to fly? said the penguin,
I just can't keep up,
I don't know what we'll do
If the volcanoes erupt.

How to fly? said the penguin
engines and metal wings
but they destroy the planet
all those human things.

How to fly? said the penguin
we should leave it to the birds
but with less of them around
we should trust God's word.

I'm a bird, said the penguin,
Why can't I fly?
We shouldn't mess with nature
and let out a small sigh.

Ben Brown (13)
The Cotswold School, Bourton-on-the-Water

Pollution, Pollution, Pollution

Pollution, pollution, pollution,
That's a well known word,
Yet, it seems to be ignored,
Why do people not care? It's absurd.
The world used to be a pretty place,
So happy and full of glee
But now that's gone down the pan,
And now it's up to me!

Litter is all around us,
Building up each day,
People just weave around it,
Don't pick up, but walk away.
People arguing in their cars,
Melting our planet,
I know we have to drive to places
But sometimes we can walk it.

Think of the future,
We must be aware,
For the sake of our children,
Will our planet be there?

Becky Emes (14)
The Cotswold School, Bourton-on-the-Water

Warnings

We have lived with sky over our head,
But if we don't clean up we'll all be dead,
With our bottles, packets and cans,
We could be saved with windmills and fans.
We won't just have lots of bills,
Not while the greenhouse continually fills.
Now we have a chance to stop CO_2 swarming,
You, me and everyone else can stop global warming.
So use the three Rs to keep clean, come and take this chance,
We all can save the planet, with your assistance.

Annie Riach (12)
Whitecross High School, Hereford

Me, The Parrot

Here I am,
Sitting around,
In my cage,
On the ground.

All I remember,
Was flying through the trees,
The sun in my face,
And a little warm breeze.

My friends waiting,
By a cloud,
They make me feel special,
They make me feel proud.

But now I am here
I wish to be free
To join my friends again
So I can be happy

Finally it came
My wish has come true
I have been let free
My life is now new.

Lauren Marissa Taylor (11)
Whitecross High School, Hereford

The Three Rs But Better

Reduce what you use,
Reuse what you buy,
Recycle what you have,
The more people following the code,
Recycle a load,
Reduce and reuse their stuff
Then nobody will need to huff and puff.

Sarah Mann (12)
Whitecross High School, Hereford

The Rainforest

Hear the sounds of the rainforest
The chattering birds, the howling monkeys
A painter's palette of colours.
But through the trees you will see,
Monstrous machines destroying this beautiful home.

The deafening whirring of the giant saws,
Chopping down the trees
The rumbling engines of the bulldozers,
Flattening anything in their path;
Animals and trees alike.

If we don't stop this dastardly deed,
Then all the animals will be gone and
The rainforest will be dull, silent, colourless, lifeless.
And after the rainforests, what's next?

Madeleine Roffey (11)
Whitecross High School, Hereford

War

The war is starting
Everyone's hearts are breaking
People are dying
People are crying

Buildings being destroyed
Houses being destroyed
Bombs landing
Bombs exploding
Nothing left
No one left

How do we stop it?
We fight back
But should we?
If we do we could win
But what if we lose?

Jack Stenhouse (12)
Whitecross High School, Hereford

The Fishy

Coke, lemonade, orange juice,
All these tons of rubbish.
Paper, card, chocolate mouse
There's more and more each day.

Swim, swim, dodge the litter,
Don't get caught up in it
It makes me feel so bitter
Why do people do it?

Day after day
When will it stop?
Never being able to glide and play
What's the point in it?

Just stop this please
If I had them
I'd beg on my knees
It makes us float to the surface.

Laura Watson (12)
Whitecross High School, Hereford

Being Homeless

I feel sad and worthless as I sit and beg.
If only I had a home,
I wish I had a family
I feel so alone.

No drink for me to drink,
Nothing for me to eat,
Because I can't afford food,
People's remarks are so crude.

Lots of dirty looks from passers-by
No one would know or care if I die.
I would fly up to Heaven in the sky.
At least then I would be at peace.
Hopefully one day people living on the streets will cease.

Emilia Booth (12)
Whitecross High School, Hereford

Animal Extinction, Polar Bear Poem!

Ever wondered about a polar bear
And the big fur coat they wear?
Their white coat keeps them in disguise,
From evil hunting guys.

Even though they are cute,
We have pressed mute,
On all the badness,
And the sadness.

Never neglect,
Because you will regret,
Harming a polar bear,
For a fur coat to wear

They live in the North Pole,
A place where you wouldn't catch a mole,
When they eat seals,
You can hear their little tiny squeals.

We can all pitch in to help,
Then we won't hear them yelp,
For the safety of a home,
Please help get their problems known.

Vicki Jones (12)
Whitecross High School, Hereford

Recycle, Reduce, Respect

Recycle, reduce, respect,
Help us however you can.
Recycle cardboard, cans and plastic
Reduce the waste
And respect our planet
Recycle, reduce, respect.

Mia Leak (12)
Whitecross High School, Hereford

Being Homeless

As yet another family goes by
Here I am
Cold and alone
Nearly naked

I go rummaging through the bins
To find anything
Including mouldy bags
Of chips

I'm lonely and tired
I need a drink
People are going by
As I sit and stare

I hold a cup
To see if anyone can help
This is so boring
I feel so alone

I count my coppers
Have I enough for a drink?
Yes thank goodness
I can get a can of Coke!

Lewis Pearce (12)
Whitecross High School, Hereford

As The World Dies!

As the world changes there is more pollution;
If we get together we'll have a solution;
We'll stop the fish from dying;
We'll stop them from frying;
It will stop the water getting dirty
It's a better world when you turn thirty.

William Penson (12)
Whitecross High School, Hereford

Litter

Litter, litter is so bitter.
Making us feel even sicker,
Dirty, smelly and disgusting,
Our environment needs adjusting.

It's harming lots of the creatures,
'Don't forget all you teachers'
With our plastic bags and wrappers,
They make very good trappers.

Litter, litter is so bitter,
Making us feel even sicker,
Dirty, smelly and disgusting,
Our environment needs adjusting.

If rubbish is what you recycle,
It could become your next bicycle,
If you can't be bothered to take it to a centre,
Then put it in a bin to be sorted later.

Litter, litter is so bitter.
Making us feel even sicker,
Dirty, smelly and disgusting,
Our environment needs adjusting.

Litter causes some pollution,
This isn't a good solution,
Creating a harmful course,
This unleashes a terrible force.

Litter, litter is so bitter.
Making us feel even sicker,
Dirty, smelly and disgusting,
Our environment needs adjusting.

It makes our gardens look ugly,
All the litterbugs smile smugly,
All we have to do is keep it clean,
And then we can admire the beautiful scene.

Litter, litter is so bitter.
Making us feel even sicker,
Dirty, smelly and disgusting,
Our environment needs adjusting.

Jordan Briscoe (12)
Whitecross High School, Hereford

Trees

Trees are big
Trees are tall
Don't cut them down
We need them all

Sheets of paper
Cardboard too
Can be recycled
And made brand new

They give us air
They give us wood
Don't cut too many
It isn't good

Home to creatures
Mostly small
Don't chop them down
We'll kill them all

Trees are big
Trees are tall
As years pass
We'll need them more.

Adam Williams (12)
Whitecross High School, Hereford

Life On The Streets

When people walk past, I get dirty looks,
I'm fed up with reading books,
You can smell me from a mile away,
I get about £2 a day.

I wear the same clothes as I beg each day,
I like it in May,
Because it's warm and not much rain,
All I feel is pain.

I don't have money to buy food,
People who pass are so rude,
I get sad when I think of people warm,
All my belongings are torn.

My throat gets so dry,
All I want to do is cry,
The smell of the food that I cannot buy,
People just keep on walking by.

I feel so upset,
Especially when I'm in the wet,
I wish that I lived in a house,
I wish I was with someone else.

Jess Preece (12)
Whitecross High School, Hereford

Recycling/Pollution

Recycling
Earth-saving, energy-saving
Saving, working, making
Stops pollution, saves the world
Ruining, killing, dying
Worse, starving
Pollution.

Felix Rogers (12)
Whitecross High School, Hereford

Make Poverty History

M ake poverty history forever
A frican children die every day
K illings happen during hard times
E veryone knows how to stop this altogether

P eople are dying every day
O ur country is helping all it can
V ery many people risk their lives
E veryone should stand up and be a man
R ighteousness we all should have
T ry as we might to lose this forever
Y ou and me are in this together.

H urricanes happen all the time
I n many countries that we love
S o do something about it
T orture is what they go through
O ver and over again
R ubbish is left and cities destroyed
Y ou can make a difference, go on give it a try.

Caitlin Chilman (12)
Whitecross High School, Hereford

Saving Rainforest

Saving rainforest that's my thing
Going to save the world make it a better place.
The animals need a home, a place to live.
The trees give us oxygen to help us live.
But people come along and cut them up.
Only for building, ruining our world.
The oil they get will only spoil
The world that we live in
So that's my story.

Alex Martin (12)
Whitecross High School, Hereford

Penguin Poem

The penguin race is dying out
Due to global warming
All the penguins are shouting out
We are now not forming.

They slip and slide upon the ice
Having lots of fun
Soon there will be ice no more
Oh what a bum.

Now the poles are harshly melting
They used to be very thick
They're melting down day by day
They're going so damn quick.

Hallum Prendergast (12)
Whitecross High School, Hereford

War

Why can't we have peace?
Last week I lost my niece
War is very bad
It makes everyone feel sad.

Why can't we get along?
We always have to fight
Every time we see each other
We shoot at first sight.

We use too much pollution
It's not good for the Earth
When we drop all the bombs
We ruin all the turf.

Aaron Gilligan (11)
Whitecross High School, Hereford

Global War

War, war why does it have to be?
We all say we want peace.
But it never comes through.
So why does war need to be?

We always have wars.
Many people dying.
Many people crying.
So why does war need to be?

So come on now.
Let's make peace today!
Turn the world to peace.
So burn the weapons today.

Lewis Rogers (12)
Whitecross High School, Hereford

Death

Is peace so hard?
No one can do it.
Death's too easy
'Cause everyone can

We create a war
Just to kill
We need more peace
To heal the ill

Peace is good
Death is bad
Peace is great
Death is mad.

Jack Parkes (12)
Whitecross High School, Hereford

The Life Of A Turtle

Swimming all day makes me hungry and sad,
When there is no food you could never be glad.
All my family has gone
So that makes me the only one.

Searching for food all through the day
I can never tell if I'm going the right way
I hope for food, I wish and wish
All I want is a little fish.

All there is, is food and drink
Just left to sink
That's why my family went to Heaven
My little brother was only seven.

Maybe I should take a bite
Even though it will give me a fright
Please stop and change the world now
You know how.

Poppy Williams (12)
Whitecross High School, Hereford

War!

As yet another bomb drops,
And the flesh takes 5 more bullets,
Hell is still here on Earth,
And one more body drops to the dirt.

This is destroying all our land,
As crops blow up,
And no one's left to stand,
Our world's in deep trouble.

But we can stop this,
Try and create no more weapons,
So our world can live in peace,
For once . . .

Jack Allen (12)
Whitecross High School, Hereford

The Cruel, Cruel World

Poverty is full of hate,
Alone, sad, without a mate,
Poor and hungry, homeless and frightened,
Is there no stop to this cruelty?
Just think how lucky you are,
To have friends and family who will go afar,
To love you, help you and care for you,
Think of all the girls and boys,
Working hard, with no reward.
They are as young as five or six
Rummaging through garbage, for money and food.
Is there no stop in this cruel, cruel world?
It happens in Africa, Britain, Japan,
Everywhere people are suffering.
Whether it's abuse, starvation or homelessness,
All they need is a warm heart.
But just remember, think of this and say,
You are lucky, every day.
With warmth and love, food and drink,
Give up some time to sit down and think.

Naomi Kemp (12)
Whitecross High School, Hereford

Recycle More

R euse, reduce, recycle
E nergy-saving
C omposting
Y ou can do it!
C leaner world
L et's all pull together
E co-friendly

M agnificent planet
O zone layer needs help
R espect our Earth
E veryone can do it, if we all work together.

Kori Lee (12)
Whitecross High School, Hereford

Bless The Homeless

Think how lucky you are to have a room to stay,
The homeless are looked at millions of times a day.
People think they are really rough, which isn't very fair,
Don't judge a book by its cover, they are human like us.
They eat scraps,
While we sit down and have proper food.
God bless them.
We need to do something to help,
They cry and beg for money,
They wish for a better life
People walk by and trash their bed and blankets
We hardly ever think about them.
What I'm trying to say,
Is get them back on their feet
Give them something to really make their day.

Carys Kenyon (12)
Whitecross High School, Hereford

Save The World

Don't fight,
Just because it's not right.
Resolve it in a better way.

Stop cutting down trees,
You're killing homes,
Become greener every day.

Stop using your car,
Polluting the world,
Walking is just as good.

Don't stay in your house,
Go out and about,
Get involved with your neighbourhood.

Oliver Deakin (12)
Whitecross High School, Hereford

My Recycling Poem

Use solar power
It's really, really good.
Recycle old newspaper,
You know you should,
Do recycle more
For the planet floor
Use your feet don't,
I say don't, drive,
And please
Save the bee hives,
If this poem did not hit you,
Nothing else will . . .
So listen
Save our planet!

Jordan Lambourn (11)
Whitecross High School, Hereford

Big Green Poetry Machine

Recycling is so fun
Once you get it done
Everyone can recycle
Try and stop pollution.

You can recycle cans
Even pots and pans
Try and recycle paper
Don't leave it till later.

Try and save the trees
Oh help us would you please.

Holly Weaver (11)
Whitecross High School, Hereford

Let's Change Poverty To Equality

L et's change poverty to equality
E very person in the world should have shelter
T he world needs to help others
S ome people won't eat tonight.

C an we do this some may ask
H ere is where the future starts
A fter time we'll complete the task
N othing can stop us now
G et the word out, spread it around
E ventually it will be found.

P eople need to take a stand
O ur word is true
V ictory! Change poverty
E quality is what we need
R ead it in the papers
T he government is where it starts
Y ou should help too!

T ell everybody in the world
O ne country is not enough.

E very country needs to change
Q uestions need to be answered
U nderstanding is what we need
A nswers need to be found
L et's all find the solution
I have a dream
T o change poverty to equality
Y es, yes, yes!

Abbie Blake (12)
Whitecross High School, Hereford

Respect

Respect is not to drop rubbish
So don't be so sluggish
Saving the planet is an easy thing to do
Keeping everything clean
So the Earth will gleam
Respect is about being able to listen
And not to respond too soon
There is no respect if the world is filled with gloom!
Respect is not to hold someone in awe
But to listen and discuss what you saw
I respect my family
Because they respect me too!

Tyler Westlake (12)
Whitecross High School, Hereford

What Have We Done?

Fire blazing everywhere,
Animals going afar,
Trees and life are dying as we know it.
Birds fly high but chicks, they perish,
Small rodents aren't safe,
They're trapped in the flames
And this is because of you
So think
Stop
You're not just killing the animals
You're killing the planet too!

Charley-Jennifer Mead (12)
Whitecross High School, Hereford

Homelessness

You see them on the street
They sit there begging for money
In filthy rags they stare at you
And you stare at them.

Give them some money
Offer them a home
Help them in some way
And save the Earth

God's gift
Depends on us
We must be respectful
And treat all equally.

Lucien Barsacq (12)
Whitecross High School, Hereford

Stop The Crime

Vandalism, trespassing, violence, theft and murder.
All these crimes are serious, you may even be the victim.
They're always happening all the time, make sure you don't forget.
If you give victims some support they will all feel much better.

Adam Andrews (12)
Whitecross High School, Hereford

Peace

Peace is a bird tweeting in its bird bath
Peace is a happy person walking home
Peace is a piece of cake filled with joy
Peace is an arm that's never been harmed
Peace is a group of friends getting along.

Emma Alty (12)
Whitecross High School, Hereford

What I've Done

As life changes and the ozone weakens,
The ice caps melt and wildlife flee their habitats
People are left homeless after floods wash their homes away,
We continue to spoil the world for future generations,
Life is changing as we know it, the world is changing,
Act now!

Joshua Rees (12)
Whitecross High School, Hereford

Animals' Extinction

Elephants running around, scared and frightened,
Wondering what's going to happen next,
People hunting them just for their ivory,
Why do they, why?
Other animals just getting killed for nothing,
Does this world have any sense?
Why do they, why?

Harriet Hodnett (11)
Wigmore High School, Leominster

Racism

R acist people are really bad,
A nd they also make people really sad,
C alling people mean names,
I diots think they're playing games,
S top this stupid nasty thing,
M any people are crying.

Steve Juson (12)
Wigmore High School, Leominster

The Green Poetry Machine

T igers are getting shot
H orses are getting pretty hot
E agles are falling from the sky

G rasshoppers jump nice and high
R abbits like to lie under the sky
E lephants are in a stampede
E els have a lot of speed
N ewts are very small when they're born

P arrots fly right up to the sky
O tters jump out the water pretty high
E lectric eels are very nasty
T arantulas are very ghastly
R ats are pretty scary
Y aks are very hairy

M ice are getting killed by mouse traps
A nts are getting eaten by other predators
C ats are getting killed by cars
H ares are getting eaten by foxes
I guanas are getting killed by pollution
N orthern tigers are getting hunted
E lectric eels are dying out.

Josh Barber (12)
Wigmore High School, Leominster

Save The Animals!

A shame the world's becoming this,
N o more polluting can save so much,
I t's killing animals and the environment,
M y opinion should be like yours,
A ll the animals slowly dying,
L itter kills animals too,
S ave the animals!

Elliot Sparrow (12)
Wigmore High School, Leominster

Say No To Nuclear Power

When we first split the atom,
We thought we were doing good.
But it didn't turn out that way,
I never thought it would.

Nuclear power is dangerous,
It makes atomic bombs,
You drop them out of aeroplanes,
Millions die with aplomb.

It's made of very lethal things,
Uranium, radon and other pieces.
It spreads around us as if it has wings,
Causing death and destruction wherever it goes.

Nuclear power should go,
We've better things to use,
We'll use wind power as it blows,
Nuclear power, no thanks,
Nuclear power, definitely no thanks.

Jack Clayton (11)
Wigmore High School, Leominster

A Bird!

Once a bird sang a song,
His tail feathers were very long,
He lived in a tree far away,
He enjoyed his life every day,
One day people came along,
And chopped down all he had to belong,
No tree was left,
He was bereft,
Rainforest gone, nothing to see,
Poor old bird, dead was he.

Heulwen Gilbert (12)
Wigmore High School, Leominster

The Pain Of The Homeless

There they sit alone and cold trying to make fires out of chunks of coal.
They scream and cry, while we stand close by.
We turn away when they look in our eyes, for we can't cope with the
pain of thinking they're humans that can hardly survive.
They pass away, when life gets bad, how can we be there
                                            and not get sad?
There are parents and children, children and parents
It doesn't make a difference because there is a solution.
Try giving money, food and water because the less you give the more
they get poorer.

Danielle Johnston (12)
Wigmore High School, Leominster

Before And After

The polar bear: With bright amber eyes; strong paws; rich, heavy fur.
Teeth glint and paws gleam.

The polar bear: With blank, lifeless eyes; tired paws; dull, drooping fur.
Teeth clenched and claws blunt.

And just imagine . . . all because of people like you.

Laura Johnson (12)
Wigmore High School, Leominster

I'm Alone

I'm alone, haven't got a home
I went bankrupt because our government is corrupt.
I haven't got any friends, I feel like life is going to end.
I wish someone would help me, I want to be with my family.
They have a home, God, I'm so alone.

Jordan Bufton (12)
Wigmore High School, Leominster

Please Help!

People killing, children dying
People hurting, hear them crying.
Please help, take a minute now and then.
Take time to remember the waste of good men.
People hurting, children crying.

Why do people fight?
Do they think it's right?
People killing, people dying.

Give to charity, peace serenity,
Talk to soldiers, help them see.
They don't help make people free!
People hurting, hear them dying.

Julia Byatt (12)
Wigmore High School, Leominster

Help!

Switch off all the lights.
Be a little braver,
Save some animals' lives,
Arctic lives are going,
Faster than we think,
Poor little penguins have nowhere to stamp their feet.
Dying out of food,
Dying out of water,
Help isn't coming
So why don't we care?
So switch off all the lights,
Do the right thing,
Save penguins' lives.
Ice is melting faster.
What do we do?

Molly Bashford (12)
Wigmore High School, Leominster

Animals

I am an elephant who is very cute
At night I hear the owls hoot
Just waiting for a poacher's toot.

I lie awake till morning
And then I start yawning.
I think to myself you can help
Just stop killing me
And others as well.
They only kill me for the ivory
And I'm quite lively
I sometimes charge at humans
But I don't mean it really
Tomorrow will be another day
But I'll protect my family.

Zoe Priday (11)
Wigmore High School, Leominster

Litter

On the news the other day,
There was lots of litter on white sands bay
Bees were flying everywhere,
And people don't seem to care.
What can you do?
It's up to you,
But here are a few ideas:
Put your litter in the bin,
And a better life will begin.
Make sure you recycle your rubbish,
Because that is my wish.

Eilish Gilbert (12)
Wigmore High School, Leominster

War

Everywhere there's war,
Even though it's such a bore.
Loads of people die,
And families cry.
Why do you damage this world?
To it you cause mould.
A stupid dingy, ugly place,
This is war's case
Bombs and missiles from up high,
From these vehicles you fly,
Making stupid weaponry,
Using natural energy
Using money from banks
To make dangerous tanks.

James Phillips (12)
Wigmore High School, Leominster

Recycle Green

Don't chuck away your litter
It makes the planet bitter
Why don't you recycle your litter?
It makes the planet fitter
Plastics, metals, bottles and paper
You must not do them later
Do them soon
Or you will meet your doom
Save the Earth and be green
If you don't you're very mean.

Matthew Beaumont-Pike (11)
Wigmore High School, Leominster

Tomorrow . . .

I am a tiger,
With huge great paws of white,
I have long thin whiskers,
And prowl the jungle by night,
And think about this,
Just once or twice,
For I might not be here,
Tomorrow . . .

I am a panda,
With large black eyes,
I have a big black nose,
And am quite a fair size,
And think about this,
Just once or twice,
For I might not be here,
Tomorrow . . .

I am a monkey,
With small shiny eyes, so I can see,
I have a tiny nose,
And like to swing in the trees,
And think about this,
Just once or twice,
For I might not be here,
Tomorrow . . .

So please think about this,
Just once or twice,
For we might not be here tomorrow . . .

Rhian Stevens (12)
Wigmore High School, Leominster

Recycling, Recycling, Recycling

Recycling, recycling, it's what you need to do
No plastic bags, no smoking fags,
Down at Waterloo.

The binmen are waiting,
Horns are honking,
No one sees,
There's no recycling.

There's the bin,
All alone,
It's so tempting,
Yet so cold.

But no more rubbish,
Not for me,
The holes in the ground,
I'll set them free.

Watch them go,
Not watch them grow,
That's the way it must be.

So I'll recycle, recycle, recycle till the end,
No plastic bags, no smoking fags,
Down at Waterloo.

Amy Cave-Browne-Cave (12)
Wigmore High School, Leominster

How Life Works

War helps no more than the starving poor!
Pollution is not a good solution!
Litter is for the bitter!
Recycling helps the solution of pollution!
Climate change is trouble, same as being homeless!
We are killing animals while we are living!
Litter kills animals then extinction takes the phase
Racism, causes prison
You can't write poetry if half the world is in poverty.

Jay Thomas Warner (12)
Wigmore High School, Leominster

Young Writers Information

We hope you have enjoyed reading this book - and that you will continue to enjoy it in the coming years.

If you like reading and writing poetry drop us a line, or give us a call, and we'll send you a free information pack.

Alternatively if you would like to order further copies of this book or any of our other titles, then please give us a call or log onto our website at
www.youngwriters.co.uk

**Young Writers Information
Remus House
Coltsfoot Drive
Woodston
Peterborough
PE2 9JX**

(01733) 890066